Izon's
Backpacker Journal

TEN SPEED PRESS
BERKELEY, CALIFORNIA

First published in Canada in 1996 by L. A. Services.

Ten Speed Press
P.O. Box 7123
Berkeley, California 94707

Distributed in New Zealand by Tandem Press, in Australia by Simon and Schuster Australia, in South Africa by Real Books, in Singapore and Malaysia by Berkeley Books, and in the United Kingdom and Europe by Airlift Books.

Design by Gillian Tsintziras, The Brookview Group
Original illustrations (c) Colette Copeland
Cover photo by David Allen

Library of Congress Cataloging-in-Publication Data on file with publisher

First Printing, 1998
Printed in USA

1 2 3 4 5 6 7 8 9 10 - 02 01 00 99 98

The author and publisher have made every effort to ensure that the information provided is accurate and does not assume any liability for any loss, injury, or inconvenience sustained by any person as a result of using information or advice from this book

This journal can help you capture the most memorable moments of your adventure. Use words, sketches, picture postcards, matchbook covers, stamps, wine labels, ticket stubs, or a few grains of sand taped to a page. Record unusual cultural traditions, ask new friends to write comments, and when you get home, clip photos and add them in. This is your story; how you tell it is up to you and your imagination.

Bon Voyage
Lucy Izon

With Special thanks to Gerry Hall and
Catherine George

Eighteen years ago you took a chance and helped
a young traveller to start a newspaper column.
Without your encouragement and support this
book and many wonderful adventures would
not have been possible.

&

My sincere gratitude to the travellers
and travel writers who shared their insights
and allowed me to quote their comments.

Name: _____

Address: _____

_____

_____

Tel/Fax: _____

_____

Birth date: _____ Soc. Sec. or S.I.N. No: _____

_____

Passport: _____ Expires: _____ Place/Date Issued: _____

_____ Birth Certificate # _____

Driver's Licence: _____ International Dr. Licence: _____

Travel Agent: _____ Tel/Fax: _____

_____

Frequent Flyer Programs: _____

_____

Air/ Bus/ Rail/ Sea Tickets (Type & Numbers) _____

_____

_____

Credit Cards (Coded Numbers)   Expires   Contact if lost or stolen _____

_____

Travellers' Cheque Hotline _____

Insurance Co. _____

_____

_____ Policy Number _____

Camera Equipment Serial Numbers _____

_____

Bank: _____ Tel/Fax: _____

Notes: _____

_____

_____

_____

_____

_____

MEDICAL

In Case of Emergency Contact _____

_____

_____ Tel/Fax: _____

_____

_____ Tel/Fax: _____

_____

Physician: _____

_____

_____ Tel/Fax: _____

Blood Type: _____ Religion: _____

Allergies: _____

_____

_____

Special Medical Condition: _____

_____

_____

_____

Medications Being Taken: _____

_____

_____

Travel Inoculations: _____ Expires: _____

_____

_____

_____

_____

Eye/Contact Prescriptions: _____

_____

_____

Medical Insurance _____

_____

_____

Notes:_____

_____

_____

_____

_____

_____

PRE-TRIP PLANNING

Fill in and photocopy pages 6, 7, 12, 13, 15, 16, & 18 along with your tickets, prescriptions and passport. Leave one set at home with friends or family. Pack another separately from the original documents (or give to your travel companion).

Check medical risks and recommended precautions with a travel medical specialist. Some inoculations must be given over several weeks; some medications must be started weeks before you go. If you're going to be travelling for less than six months, go 4–6 weeks in advance. If you're going to travel for a longer period, go 8–10 weeks in advance.

If taking insulin injections or oral contraceptives get advice on taking the medication when travelling through time zones.

If you need to carry medication or a syringe, have a medical prescription from your doctor for border inspections. Medi-kits with syringes may include a certificate for your doctor to sign.

Check if your travel medical insurance excludes coverage during high-risk activities such as scuba diving, skiing, motorcycle riding, rafting, etc., or if injured as a result of an act of war. Find out the procedure for bill payment should you require medical attention abroad.

Have a dental checkup. If you have reason to suspect you might have to deal with a severely painful situation, your dentist could prescribe an antibiotic, antiinflamatory, and painkiller combination for temporary relief while you search for suitable treatment.

Check the renewal date on your passport. Some countries, such as India and Malaysia, require that visitors' passports be valid for at least six months to enter their country. If you are having a new passport photograph taken, try to look professional; it may garner you more respect with border officials.

Arranging visas can take weeks because of having to supply your passport for different applications.

Check your automobile insurance and credit card benefits to see if you have any coverage should you decide to rent.

Research your destination. Free information and maps are available from tourist information offices. Libraries are good sources for background information.

Invest in a current guidebook suited to your style of travel. Names to look for include: <u>Lonely Planet</u>, <u>Moon Publications</u>, <u>Let's Go</u> and <u>Rough Guides</u>. You'll meet some of the leading authors through quotes in this journal.

Ask your Internet service provider what information you'll need to pick up your e-mail from a foreign location. Test picking it up from a second location before you leave home.

ASK YOUR TRAVEL AGENT

Which countries charge departure taxes, and in what currency.

Which flights will need to be confirmed, and how far in advance.

If you can pre-select a comfortable seat on your flight. For really long flights, ask if there are certain days when the loads are lighter and you're more likely to get space to stretch out.

Where to register cameras and electronic equipment before you leave the country so you won't be charged duty when you bring it back home.

Where to get current information on visa requirements and medical recommendations.

AT YOUR BANK

Find out what fee is charged for obtaining cash from ATM machines abroad.

Find out the easiest way to obtain money from home.

Check what arrangements you'll need to make if you want to give someone else the power to pay your bills from your account in your absence.

Purchase travellers' cheques and obtain contact numbers to use if they are lost or stolen.

Ask if the offices affiliated with your travellers' cheques provide other services, such as holding mail. Get the addresses.

PICKING A PACK

Test packs with weights in them so you get a proper feel and fit.

A hip belt will pull the weight closer to your centre of gravity and lessen the stress on your shoulders.

The less there is hanging outside, the less there is to get caught and damaged by baggage handlers.

Make sure the pack and sidepockets can be locked, so nothing can be slipped in or out.

Add a badge or something to identify it as yours, in case there is a similar pack on any of your flights.

TRAVEL PARTNERS

Have each person make a list of the top things they want to see or do. Compare, and try to make sure everyone has an equal number of their choices addressed.

Remember, you're not joined at the hip. Sometimes it's good to spend a few hours or days apart, and have different experiences to share when you team up again.

Your gateway to Backpacker Information on the Internet
Izon's Backpacker Journal
www.izon.com

Tourism Offices Worldwide Directory
http://www.towd.com

City.Net (links to more than 5,000 cities & destinations)
http://www.city.net

Internet Guide to Hostelling (list of 3,000+ hostels)
http://www.hostels.com/hostels/

Hostelling International
http://www.iyhf.org

International Student Travel Confederation (ISTC)
(worldwide database of student discounts)
http://www.istc.org

Travel CUTS (Canadian Federation of Students)
http://www.travelcuts.com

Council on International Educational Exchange (CIEE)
http://www.ciee.org

STA Travel
http://www.sta-travel.com

Lonely Planet Publications (destination information & traveller's
bulletin board)
http://www.lonelyplanet.com

Moon Publications Online (destination & health information)
http://www.moon.com

Centers for Disease Control and Prevention (Atlanta) (traveller's health)
http://www.cdc.gov

World Weather
http://www.intellicast.com/weather/intl

US State Department Travel Warnings
http://www.travel.state.gov/travel_warnings.html

Canadian Govt. Travel Information and Advisory Reports
http://www.dfait-maeci.gc.ca

Australian Consular Travel Advice
http://www.dfat.gov.au/consular

1998

JANUARY
```
S  M  T  W  T  F  S
            1  2  3
4  5  6  7  8  9  10
11 12 13 14 15 16 17
18 19 20 21 22 23 24
25 26 27 28 29 30 31
```

FEBRUARY
```
S  M  T  W  T  F  S
1  2  3  4  5  6  7
8  9  10 11 12 13 14
15 16 17 18 19 20 21
22 23 24 25 26 27 28
```

MARCH
```
S  M  T  W  T  F  S
1  2  3  4  5  6  7
8  9  10 11 12 13 14
15 16 17 18 19 20 21
22 23 24 25 26 27 28
29 30 31
```

APRIL
```
S  M  T  W  T  F  S
         1  2  3  4
5  6  7  8  9  10 11
12 13 14 15 16 17 18
19 20 21 22 23 24 25
26 27 28 29 30
```

MAY
```
S  M  T  W  T  F  S
               1  2
3  4  5  6  7  8  9
10 11 12 13 14 15 16
17 18 19 20 21 22 23
24 25 26 27 28 29 30
31
```

JUNE
```
S  M  T  W  T  F  S
   1  2  3  4  5  6
7  8  9  10 11 12 13
14 15 16 17 18 19 20
21 22 23 24 25 26 27
28 29 30
```

JULY
```
S  M  T  W  T  F  S
         1  2  3  4
5  6  7  8  9  10 11
12 13 14 15 16 17 18
19 20 21 22 23 24 25
26 27 28 29 30 31
```

AUGUST
```
S  M  T  W  T  F  S
                  1
2  3  4  5  6  7  8
9  10 11 12 13 14 15
16 17 18 19 20 21 22
23 24 25 26 27 28 29
30 31
```

SEPTEMBER
```
S  M  T  W  T  F  S
      1  2  3  4  5
6  7  8  9  10 11 12
13 14 15 16 17 18 19
20 21 22 23 24 25 26
27 28 29 30
```

OCTOBER
```
S  M  T  W  T  F  S
            1  2  3
4  5  6  7  8  9  10
11 12 13 14 15 16 17
18 19 20 21 22 23 24
25 26 27 28 29 30 31
```

NOVEMBER
```
S  M  T  W  T  F  S
1  2  3  4  5  6  7
8  9  10 11 12 13 14
15 16 17 18 19 20 21
22 23 24 25 26 27 28
29 30
```

DECEMBER
```
S  M  T  W  T  F  S
      1  2  3  4  5
6  7  8  9  10 11 12
13 14 15 16 17 18 19
20 21 22 23 24 25 26
27 28 29 30 31
```

1999

JANUARY
```
S  M  T  W  T  F  S
               1  2
3  4  5  6  7  8  9
10 11 12 13 14 15 16
17 18 19 20 21 22 23
24 25 26 27 28 29 30
31
```

FEBRUARY
```
S  M  T  W  T  F  S
   1  2  3  4  5  6
7  8  9  10 11 12 13
14 15 16 17 18 19 20
21 22 23 24 25 26 27
28
```

MARCH
```
S  M  T  W  T  F  S
   1  2  3  4  5  6
7  8  9  10 11 12 13
14 15 16 17 18 19 20
21 22 23 24 25 26 27
28 29 30 31
```

APRIL
```
S  M  T  W  T  F  S
            1  2  3
4  5  6  7  8  9  10
11 12 13 14 15 16 17
18 19 20 21 22 23 24
25 26 27 28 29 30
```

MAY
```
S  M  T  W  T  F  S
                  1
2  3  4  5  6  7  8
9  10 11 12 13 14 15
16 17 18 19 20 21 22
23 24 25 26 27 28 29
30 31
```

JUNE
```
S  M  T  W  T  F  S
      1  2  3  4  5
6  7  8  9  10 11 12
13 14 15 16 17 18 19
20 21 22 23 24 25 26
27 28 29 30
```

JULY
```
S  M  T  W  T  F  S
            1  2  3
4  5  6  7  8  9  10
11 12 13 14 15 16 17
18 19 20 21 22 23 24
25 26 27 28 29 30 31
```

AUGUST
```
S  M  T  W  T  F  S
1  2  3  4  5  6  7
8  9  10 11 12 13 14
15 16 17 18 19 20 21
22 23 24 25 26 27 28
29 30 31
```

SEPTEMBER
```
S  M  T  W  T  F  S
         1  2  3  4
5  6  7  8  9  10 11
12 13 14 15 16 17 18
19 20 21 22 23 24 25
26 27 28 29 30
```

OCTOBER
```
S  M  T  W  T  F  S
               1  2
3  4  5  6  7  8  9
10 11 12 13 14 15 16
17 18 19 20 21 22 23
24 25 26 27 28 29 30
31
```

NOVEMBER
```
S  M  T  W  T  F  S
   1  2  3  4  5  6
7  8  9  10 11 12 13
14 15 16 17 18 19 20
21 22 23 24 25 26 27
28 29 30
```

DECEMBER
```
S  M  T  W  T  F  S
      1  2  3  4
5  6  7  8  9  10 11
12 13 14 15 16 17 18
19 20 21 22 23 24 25
26 27 28 29 30 31
```

2000

JANUARY
```
S  M  T  W  T  F  S
                  1
2  3  4  5  6  7  8
9  10 11 12 13 14 15
16 17 18 19 20 21 22
23 24 25 26 27 28 29
30 31
```

FEBRUARY
```
S  M  T  W  T  F  S
      1  2  3  4  5
6  7  8  9  10 11 12
13 14 15 16 17 18 19
20 21 22 23 24 25 26
27 28 29
```

MARCH
```
S  M  T  W  T  F  S
         1  2  3  4
5  6  7  8  9  10 11
12 13 14 15 16 17 18
19 20 21 22 23 24 25
26 27 28 29 30 31
```

APRIL
```
S  M  T  W  T  F  S
                  1
2  3  4  5  6  7  8
9  10 11 12 13 14 15
16 17 18 19 20 21 22
23 24 25 26 27 28 29
30
```

MAY
```
S  M  T  W  T  F  S
      1  2  3  4  5
6  7  8  9  10 11 12
13 14 15 16 17 18 19
20 21 22 23 24 25 26
27 28 29 30 31
```

JUNE
```
S  M  T  W  T  F  S
            1  2  3
4  5  6  7  8  9  10
11 12 13 14 15 16 17
18 19 20 21 22 23 24
25 26 27 28 29 30
```

JULY
```
S  M  T  W  T  F  S
                  1
2  3  4  5  6  7  8
9  10 11 12 13 14 15
16 17 18 19 20 21 22
23 24 25 26 27 28 29
30 31
```

AUGUST
```
S  M  T  W  T  F  S
      1  2  3  4  5
6  7  8  9  10 11 12
13 14 15 16 17 18 19
20 21 22 23 24 25 26
27 28 29 30 31
```

SEPTEMBER
```
S  M  T  W  T  F  S
               1  2
3  4  5  6  7  8  9
10 11 12 13 14 15 16
17 18 19 20 21 22 23
24 25 26 27 28 29 30
```

OCTOBER
```
S  M  T  W  T  F  S
1  2  3  4  5  6  7
8  9  10 11 12 13 14
15 16 17 18 19 20 21
22 23 24 25 26 27 28
29 30 31
```

NOVEMBER
```
S  M  T  W  T  F  S
         1  2  3  4
5  6  7  8  9  10 11
12 13 14 15 16 17 18
19 20 21 22 23 24 25
26 27 28 29 30
```

DECEMBER
```
S  M  T  W  T  F  S
               1  2
3  4  5  6  7  8  9
10 11 12 13 14 15 16
17 18 19 20 21 22 23
24 25 26 27 28 29 30
31
```

ITINERARY NOTES—FOLLOWING PAGES

If there are not enough spaces for the number of days you'll be travelling, tape in extra photocopied pages before you start.Work in pencil.

Note:
- Locations & dates of mail pickups
- Weekends/holidays when many banks & businesses are closed
- Where you'll need airport departure tax in local currency
- When you'll need to reconfirm next flight
- Days you need to take medication
- Events to try to attend

Remember, if you arrange to arrive early in the day you'll have the widest choice of budget accommodation.

Major museums are often closed for one day early in the week so check your guidebook in advance if your visit will be short.

Also consider reserving beds, and seats on buses and trains, in advance if arriving during major celebrations.

Don't push to see so much that the trip becomes a blur and you risk getting sick. Plan down time, especially if you are travelling in hot climates. Give yourself a chance to absorb your surroundings.

Avoid scheduling domestic air travel too close to your return international flight. A few hours of fog could cause you to miss your connection.

Date	Transportation/Place	Notes

PHOTOCOPY & KEEP

Date	Transportation/Place	Notes

Packing
Things to Consider:

A lock. You can use it on hostel lockers, and it's handy to secure luggage to racks on trains and buses.

Shoes/boots that are worn-in.

A fire-safe immersion heater that will shut off on its own if it's forgotton and overheats.

Eyeshades and earplugs for shared dormitory rooms and overnight buses.

Your old familiar cold medications for travel off the beaten track.

Patterned clothes. They won't show stains or wear as fast as plain fabrics.

Clothes that can be layered, rather than bulky items. Wool, because it will retain body heat even when damp.

A sarong, because it can also be used as a beach mat, towel, bathing suit cover-up, or to drape over your head and shoulders at a religious site.

A long-sleeved top, long pants, and a mosquito net for areas where malaria is a risk.

Cheap plastic sandals for pebble beaches and shared shower rooms.

A whistle for cycling, hiking, or as street safety alarm.

String, rope, or twine for wrapping parcels, or hanging mosquito nets or damp clothes.

Resealable plastic bags for carrying food, storing damp clothes, and protecting cameras from dust.

Large plastic garbage bags to line a pack in damp weather, to line a sink if the plug is missing, or to wear over your upper body in a downpour.

Photos of your family and postcards of your city for conversation items with foreign residents.

A flashlight or candle for power blackouts in Third-World countries.

A plastic poncho for keeping dry when walking or cycling, or for use as a groundsheet for picnics, etc.

A day pack of sturdy material with a zipper than can lock. Travellers have reported having lightweight day packs and fanny packs razored by thieves in crowded situations.

A universal sink plug so you can handwash clothes, because plugs are often missing in budget hotel rooms and at campgrounds.

A sheet sleeping bag, because, for sanitary reasons, many hostels will not allow the use of traditional sleeping bags. You can make your own by folding a sheet in half and sewing it along the bottom and up the side.

For extensive travel, you may be able to get better quality detailed maps of Third-World countries before you leave home. Inquire at bookstores that specalize in travel.

* Put your name and address inside your luggage and camera and eyeglass cases.

Quito, Ecuador - "I would really recommend that people bring a flashlight. I didn't know that they were going to shut the power off in our hotel at 11 PM."
— Karen Best, Calgary, Alberta

Packing List
The Essentials:

• • • • • • • • • • • • • • • • • • • •

passport

visas

immunization record

airline • ship • rail • bus tickets

medical • cancellation insurance

travellers' cheques • hotline phone number

guidebook

Izon's Backpacker Journal • pen

student (ISIC)/youth/senior/teacher identity card

glasses/contact lenses

photocopies of documents

money belt/pouch

toothbrush • paste

soap • shampoo

razor • shaving cream

T-shirts • sweater • rain poncho • jacket pants • underwear

socks • walking shoes/hiking boots

medi-kit • medications • prescriptions

hat • sunglasses • sunscreen

camera • film

The following is a list of other possibilities. What you'll need for your trip depends on your style of travel and your destinations. Check off what you plan to take (in pencil), then recheck when it's actually packed.

Remember, the advice most often offered by experienced travellers is to pack half the clothes, twice the money, and plenty of film. After a few weeks of toting your pack through crowded railway stations over cobbled streets and up a few steep paths, you'll regret every unnecessary ounce.

Paperwork

automobile club card
driver's licence
international drivers' permit
maps
embassy addresses (check guidebook)
foreign dictionary/phrasebook
hostel membership
baggage insurance
reading material
direct dial telephone numbers
job reference letter
photos of family & home, and photos
for visas

Money

foreign currency
credit cards
replacement hotline number
ATM card

Hardware

watch
travel alarm
flashlight/candle
Swiss Army Knife (with corkscrew,
bottle & can opener)
sink stopper
adaptor plugs • voltage convertor
combination lock • bike chain
iron/steamer
immersion heater/hot pot
spare batteries
whistle • compass
heat pads
water bottle
hair dryer
CD/tape player
binoculars

Toiletries

ear plugs
eyeshades
toilet paper (crush it)
tissue
hair conditioner
manicure kit
safety pins
tampons/sanitary napkins
condoms/contraceptives
shower cap
sunburn lotion • lip balm
insect repellent
pre-moistened towelettes
dental floss
mouthwash

wash cloth • towel
moisture lotion
deodorant
brush • comb

Medical

spare eyeglasses/prescription
adhesive & sensor bandages
medi-kit with syringe for diabetics
antidiarrhea medicine
aspirin • pain reliever
motion sickness medication
vitamins
Medic Alert identification
water purification kit/tablets
mole skin • blister pads
thermometer
cold/cough remedies
antibiotic cream
decongestant
antifungal foot powder
throat lozenges
vitamins
tweezers • fold-up scissors

Camera

camera batteries
flash
lens cleaning kit

Clothes

plastic sandals
scarf • sarong
thermal underwear
shorts • skirt
long-sleeved shirts
swim suit/cap

Other

resealable bags • large garbage bags
sleeping bag/sheet sleeping bag
tent • mattress pad
mosquito net
clothesline/pins • detergent
luggage tags
gifts
sewing kit (in empty film canister)
inflatable neck rest
twine/string/rope
knife • fork • spoon • chopsticks
matches (in hand luggage)
chewing gum
day pack

Add Your own Items

LOADING UP

Don't ever store valuables in outside pack pockets where they are out of your vision but within reach of a pickpocket.

If you put your belongings in clear plastic bags (underwear in one, shirts in another, etc.) it will be easier to unload and find things quickly.

Put containers of fluids into resealable bags in case they leak.

If you always store things in the same place it will be easier to notice if something is missing.

Pack the things you're most likely to need first on the top.

You'll find your backpack most comfortable if you keep the weight high but below the shoulders. The weight should be lowered when walking over rugged ground to improve your balance. Crossing rivers, consider undoing your hip belt so you're not pulled under if you fall in.

Try a test walk. Remove anything you don't need.

* Rip off any old airline tags.

Items Airlines Don't Want You to Pack
Because variations in temperature and air pressure can cause some items to leak or ignite, restrictions usually include: matches and lighters (in baggage), fuel, solvents, lighter refills, camping gas, adhesives, flares, bleaches and many aerosols. Look for details with your flight ticket.

Hand Luggage
Carry your passport, tickets, money, and credit cards in a money pouch under your clothing.

Keep electronic equipment and batteries in hand luggage to avoid possible time-consuming searches at airport check-in counters.

Hand-carry prescriptions and medications, and keep the medications in their original containers. Border officials are used to seeing travellers with antibiotics and malaria medication, but any narcotic (even sleeping pills) should be accompanied by a letter from your doctor.

Consider carrying anything you would need to get by for the first 24 hours if your luggage was lost.

Carry your film canisters in a clear plastic bag because airport security personnel are usually more receptive to requests for hand inspections, rather than shooting them through the X-ray machine.

Get into the habit of counting the number of items you carry on board (day pack, jacket, etc.) and making sure you have the same number when you get off.

TRAVELLER'S CHEQUES

Number	Amount	Date Cashed	Rate	Place Cashed

WORLD CLIMATE — AVERAGE TEMPERATURES

CITY	Jan	Feb	Mar	Apr	May	Jun	Jul	Aug	Sept	Oct	Nov	Dec
Alice Springs	36	35	32	27	22	19	19	22	27	31	33	35
Amsterdam	03	03	05	09	14	15	17	18	16	11	07	04
Athens	09	10	12	15	20	25	27	27	24	20	15	11
Atlanta	06	08	12	16	21	25	26	26	23	17	11	07
Auckland	19	19	18	17	13	12	11	11	13	14	14	18
Bangkok	26	27	29	30	30	29	28	28	28	27	27	27
Barcelona	09	10	12	14	18	21	14	14	22	18	13	10
Beijing	05	02	05	14	20	25	26	25	20	13	04	03
Berlin	-01	0	04	08	13	16	18	17	14	09	03	01
Bogota	-01	-01	03	09	15	20	26	22	19	13	07	01
Bombay	24	24	26	28	30	29	27	27	27	28	27	26
Brisbane	29	29	27	26	23	20	20	21	24	26	27	29
Brussels	02	03	06	08	13	16	18	17	14	10	05	03
Budapest	-01	-01	07	11	17	20	22	21	18	12	06	02
Buenos Aires	23	23	21	17	13	09	10	11	13	16	20	22
Cairns	32	31	30	29	27	26	25	26	28	30	31	32
Cairo	13	14	17	21	25	27	28	28	26	24	20	15
Calcutta	20	21	21	29	30	31	31	31	30	26	24	20
Caracas	19	19	21	21	22	21	21	21	21	21	20	20
Casablanca	12	13	14	16	18	20	22	23	22	19	16	13
Colombo	26	27	27	28	29	27	27	27	27	27	26	26
Copenhagen	-01	0	02	07	12	15	18	17	16	09	04	02
Darwin	28	28	28	28	27	25	25	26	28	29	29	29
Dallas	07	10	14	18	23	27	29	29	26	20	13	09
Delhi	14	15	20	29	30	31	30	31	30	26	24	20
Dublin	05	05	06	08	11	14	15	15	13	10	07	06
Edinburgh	03	03	05	08	10	13	15	14	13	10	06	04
Frankfurt	01	03	06	10	14	18	16	18	15	09	05	02
Geneva	01	03	06	10	14	18	20	19	16	11	06	02
Glasgow	04	04	06	08	11	13	15	14	12	09	06	04
Helsinki	-06	-06	-03	03	09	13	18	16	11	05	01	-03
Hong Kong	15	15	18	21	25	27	28	28	27	25	21	17
Honolulu	22	22	23	24	25	26	27	27	27	26	25	23
Istanbul	05	05	07	12	17	21	24	24	20	16	12	08
Jakarta	26	26	27	27	27	27	27	27	27	27	27	26
Johannesburg	20	20	28	26	13	11	11	13	16	18	19	20
Kathmandu	10	12	16	19	22	24	24	24	23	20	15	11
Kuala Lumpur	27	28	28	28	28	27	27	28	28	27	27	27
Lima	23	24	24	22	19	17	17	16	17	18	19	21
Lisbon	11	12	13	14	17	20	22	22	21	17	14	14
London	04	04	07	09	12	16	18	17	15	11	07	04
Los Angeles	13	14	14	16	18	19	22	22	21	19	16	14
Madras	29	31	33	35	38	37	35	35	34	32	29	29
Madrid	04	06	09	12	16	21	24	23	19	14	08	06
Manila	26	26	28	29	29	29	28	28	28	27	27	26
Melbourne	20	20	19	16	13	11	10	11	13	15	16	18
Mexico City	12	13	16	18	19	19	17	18	18	16	14	13
Miami	20	20	22	23	26	27	28	28	27	26	22	21
Moscow	-09	-06	-04	04	13	17	19	17	11	04	-03	-08
Munich	-02	-01	03	05	12	16	17	17	13	08	03	-01
Nairobi	18	19	19	18	16	15	16	17	18	18	18	18
Nassau	22	22	23	24	26	27	27	28	28	26	24	23
New Orleans	13	14	17	21	24	27	28	28	27	22	17	13
New York	-01	0	03	09	16	21	23	23	21	15	07	02
Oslo	-04	-03	01	06	12	16	18	16	12	06	01	-02
Paris	03	04	07	11	13	17	19	18	16	11	06	04
Penang	27	28	28	28	28	28	28	27	27	27	27	27
Perth	24	24	22	19	16	14	13	13	15	16	19	22
Prague	-01	03	04	09	14	18	19	18	15	09	03	0
Quito	14	14	14	14	14	14	14	14	14	14	14	14
Rio De Janeiro	26	26	26	24	22	21	21	21	21	22	23	25
Rome	08	09	11	14	18	22	24	24	22	17	13	09
San Francisco	10	12	13	13	14	15	15	15	17	16	14	11
San Juan	24	24	24	24	26	27	27	27	27	27	26	25
Seoul	-05	-02	03	11	16	21	25	26	20	13	05	-02
Shanghai	10	11	11	19	23	25	27	28	26	23	19	14
Singapore	27	27	28	28	28	28	28	28	27	27	27	27
Stockholm	-03	-03	0	07	09	14	17	16	11	07	02	-01
Sydney	22	22	21	19	15	13	12	13	15	18	20	21
Taipei	16	15	18	21	24	27	29	28	27	23	20	17
Tel Aviv	14	14	17	19	23	26	28	28	27	25	21	16
Tokyo	03	04	07	13	17	21	25	26	22	17	11	06
Toronto	-01	-01	03	10	17	23	26	25	21	13	06	01
Vancouver	05	07	10	14	18	21	23	23	18	14	09	06
Vienna	01	01	06	12	15	19	21	20	17	11	06	01
Warsaw	06	08	12	16	21	25	26	26	23	17	11	07
Washington D.C.	01	03	07	12	18	23	25	24	20	14	08	03
Zurich	0	-01	05	09	13	16	18	18	14	09	03	01

CEL. TO FAH.
-05 — 23
-04 — 24
-03 — 26
-02 — 28
-01 — 30
0 — 32.0
01 — 33.8
02 — 35.6
03 — 37.4
04 — 39.2
05 — 41.0
06 — 42.8
07 — 44.6
08 — 46.4
09 — 48.2
10 — 50.0
11 — 51.8
12 — 53.6
13 — 55.4
14 — 57.2
15 — 59.0
16 — 60.8
17 — 62.6
18 — 64.4
19 — 66.2
20 — 68.0
21 — 69.8
22 — 71.6
23 — 73.4
24 — 75.2
25 — 77.0
26 — 78.8
27 — 80.6
28 — 82.4
29 — 84.2
30 — 86.8

TOURIST INFORMATION SERVICES

Not all are unbiased. Some are operated by cities and governments, while others will only give information about services that are paying them a fee.

CONSIDER ASKING ABOUT:

Free maps.

Areas to avoid.

Accommodation listings.

Reservations services (e.g., Copenhagen has a free youth accommodation and luggage storage service at the "Use It" office).

Transit passes and discounts.

Bank, store & business hours.

Hours of galleries' and museums' free entry.

TOURIST INFORMATION SERVICES

CONSIDER ASKING ABOUT:

Special events in the region. Meet-the-people programs (available from Japan to the Bahamas).

Homestay information (exists from India to Indonesia).

Tax refund (VAT) for shopping (it may not be worth the effort).

Departure taxes. Charged when leaving by air from many coun-tries and by bus from Israel. You may need local currency.

English-language telephone infor-mation services (e.g., they exist in Mexico and Japan).

BUDGET ACCOMMODATION

WHAT TO LOOK FOR

In addition to budget hotels, consider:

Youth hostels, which now exist in at least 60 countries. They offer inexpensive accommodation in multi-share rooms; some also have family and couples rooms. All but a few open their doors to travellers of any age.

Hostelling International (HI) is an association of 5,000 youth hostels worldwide with an international computerized reservations system. Bookings can be made in HI hostels in major gateway cities.

Independent travellers' hostels are popular and competitive around the world. Networks exist in North America, Australia, New Zealand and Ireland.

BUDGET ACCOMMODATION

YMCA and YWCA lodging centres (with beds for both men and women) exist in North America, Europe, the Middle East and the Far East.

More than 700 universities and colleges open their residences to travellers of any age during Christmas, Easter and summer holiday periods.

From Latvia to Australia and New Zealand, it's possible to stay at many campgrounds even if you don't have a tent. Inexpensive cabins or "on-site vans" are available for rent.

THE SEARCH

"We had no concrete plans for our trip and never had trouble finding lodging, even in August—Malaysia's highest tourist season. We made an effort to arrive early enough in the day at each destination, sometimes before noon, to secure a room."
– Denise Mills
Portland, Oregon

When using a popular guidebook, remember, you'll be one of many so it's especially important to get there early.

Other travellers will be your best source of current information. Ask for recommendations and note them in this journal, or the back of your guidebook.

THE SEARCH

If no beds are available in a hostel/hotel you like, ask their staff for recommendations. They may have the inside track on something just as suitable.

In some cities, such as Brisbane (at the bus terminal), there are reservation services specifically geared to backpackers.

TOUTS

From India to Athens, "touts" latch onto arriving travellers and manoeuvre them to hotels and hostels that will pay them a commission. Their help may save you time and trouble, but your rate may be raised to include the commission. If you go, see the room before you pay and only pay for one night, until you've had a chance to find out what other travellers are being charged.

Warning: At one time an IYHF youth hostel in Bangkok had to print a warning on its brochures about taxi drivers who were telling travellers the hostel had burned down so that they would be willing to be taken to a different hotel, where the driver would collect a commission.

TOUTS

"One led me to a half-finished building on the Greek island of Poros. The floors were built but the walls weren't up and the owner decided to make some money by putting in a bunch of cots and blankets separating the 'rooms.'

"I made one mistake. I didn't ask enough questions as to location and description before I went with him.

"Another time I used a tout in Toledo, Spain. He helped me locate a simple clean room, in a small medieval house in the centre of town. Never would have found that one by myself."
- Richard Trilling
Paris, France

27

ACCOMMODATION

CHECKING IT OUT

Get ready to experience new cultural traditions.
In China and Japan the toilets may be at floor-level, and in Moscow you'll probably never see a double bed; tiny twins seem to be the standard in most hotel rooms.

BEFORE CHECKING IN, LOOK FOR:

A clean bathroom and running hot water.

A room away from noisy street traffic.

If there is a rate posted on the back of the door, does it match the price you've been quoted?

ACCOMMODATION

Have you been quoted the full price? Hidden extras could include showers, taxes and compulsory meals.

If breakfast is included, find out what it consists of.

Are there proper, unblocked fire exits? Smoke detectors?

Make sure windows and doors can be secured, but easily opened if you had to get out.

Rooms by stair-ways are considered more likely to be targeted by thieves because of convenient exits.

**OFFBEAT
HOSTELS**

Using hostels can enable you to stay in some unique and unusual locations. For example:

In Stockholm, Sweden, the HI hostel is on a clipper ship in the harbor.

In Brunswick, Georgia (USA) some hostel rooms are in tree houses.

In Ottawa, Canada, travellers are accommodated in an historic jail (the beds are in the cells, bars and all).

OFFBEAT HOSTELS

In Coober Pedy, Australia, to escape the intense heat, one of the independent hostels is located underground.

In the Forest of Dean on the England/Wales border, the youth hostel is in the 1,000-year-old St. Briavels Castle. The moated Norman castle, complete with dungeon, was once used as a hunting lodge by King John.

ACCOMMODATION

SAFETY

A lock on a hotel room door doesn't ensure valuables left inside are completely secure. Use a locker or safety deposit box. Leaving items out creates temptation for low-paid staff.

You can discourage staff from entering your room when you're out by hanging a "do not disturb" sign on the door.

Credit cards stored in front-desk safety deposit boxes should be put in a sealed, signed envelope to discourage their use in your absence.

ACCOMMODATION

IN MULTI-SHARE ROOMS:

When you go to the washroom or shower keep your valuables with you. A resealable plastic bag will keep them dry.

If you don't have anywhere to lock up your valuables overnight, slide them into the bottom of your sleeping bag. Even if you trust your roommates, someone else could enter during the night and pick the place clean.

Some guides suggest you increase the security of your room at night by using a door wedge. It makes sense for robbery prevention, but it would hamper help if you were in trouble (i.e., a fire) and assistance couldn't reach you.

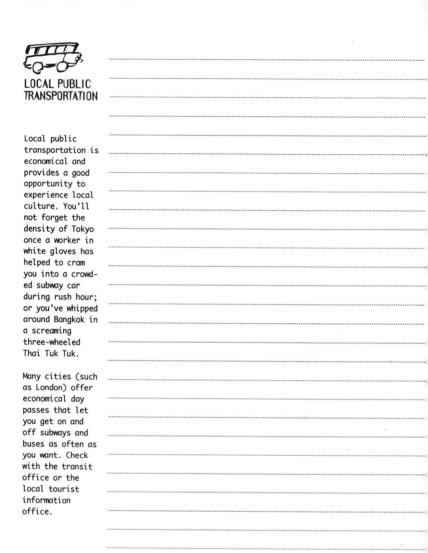

LOCAL PUBLIC TRANSPORTATION

Local public transportation is economical and provides a good opportunity to experience local culture. You'll not forget the density of Tokyo once a worker in white gloves has helped to cram you into a crowded subway car during rush hour; or you've whipped around Bangkok in a screaming three-wheeled Thai Tuk Tuk.

Many cities (such as London) offer economical day passes that let you get on and off subways and buses as often as you want. Check with the transit office or the local tourist information office.

LOCAL PUBLIC TRANSPORTATION

In some cities (such as Paris) it's cheaper to buy 10 transit tickets at a time. You can resell those you don't need to other budget travellers.

Many city transit systems operate on an honor system. Don't think that, because you're a visitor, if you're caught without a ticket you'll get off easy. Fare dodgers in London, England, for example, can be fined £200.

LOCAL TRANSPORTATION TAXIS

"In Cairo I asked a taxi driver what my fare would be to cross the city. I was quoted a price which seemed reasonable by North American standards but high for Egypt. So, I asked an Egyptian student for help. When he inquired with another driver, the fare was about one-fifth of the amount I was quoted."
– Lucy Izon

WHEN USING UNMETERED TAXIS

Ask local residents or the staff at your hotel for advice on fair rates for the distances you plan to travel.

Always settle on a fee before you begin a trip.

LOCAL TRANSPORTATION TAXIS

If possible, have a local resident help you negotiate. Writing down the rate agreed upon with a taxi or rickshaw driver and showing it to him before you start, could help avoid misunderstandings, or settle disputes if the driver tries to change the rate halfway to the destination.

Try to have small change available. Your driver may not be able to make change, or he may say he can't in order to keep the total amount.

Be wary when going to hotels or stores recommended by your driver. Chances are he's earning a commission on any money spent and prices may be inflated to cover this.

GETTING AROUND:

In countries such as Turkey, Egypt and China, citizens will offer travellers transportation in their vehicles, but be aware that it's customary to pay for this service.

"In Guatemala, after waiting most of a day for a bus, a truck driver offered us a ride. Once inside we noticed machine guns stored in the back. Later, others suggested that the drivers were probably guerillas and they picked up tourists because they would be less likely to be stopped at a road block."
— Pat Raes
Toronto, Canada

GETTING AROUND:

"Touts could save you a lot of trouble and money. Be open. Touts might help you get a ticket when all other channels fail."
– Bill Dalton
Indonesia
Handbook
Moon Publications

Crowded public buses and trains are ideal territory for pickpockets. Thieves can slice open a fanny pack or waist pouch with a razor, often without the victim noticing it. Women, espe-cially, should watch being distracted by groping hands.

BUS TRAVEL

WHAT TO TAKE:

Bottled drinking water.

If you don't have an inflatable neck rest, make your own head support by rolling a towel, pulling it around your neck, and fastening it with a safety pin.

A neck scarf can double as an eye-shade for sleeping.

Keep your sleeping bag with you in case it gets cold at night.

Earplugs can be a real blessing when you want to sleep on buses with noisy video machines.

WHICH SIDE TO SIT ON?

Check your map for the side most likely to offer interesting views.

If it's a hot climate you might want to avoid the sunny side.

BUS TRAVEL

HOW FAR BACK?

Front seats are often the most comfortable for those suffering motion sickness, and may also offer the best photographic opportunities.

In a hot climate, sitting near a ceiling vent may offer some relief.

If your luggage is stored beneath the bus, consider positioning yourself where you can keep an eye on what's being taken on and off.

On many buses you feel the bumps more in seats directly over the wheels.

When your baggage is stored out of sight on an overhead shelf or roof rack, especially on an overnight trip, see if there is a way that you can secure it with your padlock/bike chain.

BUS TRAVEL

IF YOU SUFFER FROM MOTION SICKNESS:

Avoid heavy meals but don't travel on a completely empty stomach. Crackers are usually easy on the system.

Try travelling at night when you're not as visually aware of the motion.

If you do travel in the day and you feel queasy, sit near the front and keep your eyes on the horizon.

BUS TRAVEL

A Chinese acupressure treatment for nausea and motion sickness is to grasp firmly the web of skin between the thumb and forefinger, pushing in towards the base of the finger. Hold it for several minutes.

Avoid reading.

FLYING

Airlines sometimes overbook and look for volunteers to give up their seats. Incentives can range from a night in a nice hotel to a coupon for a free flight. If the flight looks packed, let the staff know you would be willing to delay your departure for compensation.

WHERE TO SIT?

Window seats give you a wall to lean on when you sleep.

Aisle seats and seats beside emergency exits offer the most leg room.

Avoid centre seats, you may have to struggle for elbow room.

If you hope to sleep, avoid seats near washrooms and galleys, areas that are usually noisy.

FLYING

Count the number of seats to the exits in front and behind so you could find your way out if your vision was impaired.

To reduce jetlag eat light, avoid alcohol, and drink lots of water.

If you need to reconfirm your return flight, note it on your itinerary.

You may need your passport when flying domesti-cally (for example, in China), so don't leave it stored in a safe in your gateway city.

Domestic luggage weight restric-tions can differ from internation-al. To avoid surcharges carry heavier items (e.g., books) in your hand lug-gage.

RAIL - BOARDING

If you don't speak the language and need to make a reservation or complicated arrangements, have someone at your hotel/hostel write down what you want so you can show it to the ticket agent.

Head for the "right" rail station (in Europe some 70 cities have more than one station).

See if there is a sign on the platform indicating where specific cars halt, so you can board your car directly rather than squeezing your way to it along narrow hallways.

When emptying a station locker, or when boarding, be careful about setting your day pack down while securing other luggage. Thieves wait for these ideal opportunities to grab and run.

RAIL - BOARDING

Be sure you are in the right car, not just on the right train. Some trains split en route (sometimes, in the middle of the night), with cars being reattached to other trains.

Find out which is the most scenic side to sit on.

Window seats are safer for those likely to nod off because thieves would have to reach across to get at you and your belongings. You may also have the advantage of a small writing table.

RAIL - RIDING

"On the overnight train from Bangkok to Chiang Mai a security guard smiled and handed me a card. It said: "Please don't accept food or drinks from strangers, it may contain drugs". I first felt disturbed, then relieved. Instead of trying to hide their problem they were make every effort to protect the passengers."
– Lucy Izon

Always keep your money and valuable documents safely stored under your clothing.

A padlock or bicycle chain can be used to secure your pack to a rack when nodding off.

Don't ever step off the train, even for a moment, without your passport and money with you.

RAIL-RIDING

Carry your own drinking water. Most tap water on trains shouldn't even be used to brush your teeth. On Asian trains carry your own toilet paper.

If you are going to be crossing a border, spend your coins. Most foreign exchange services will not deal with them.

Some experts feel that you are less likely to have your sleeping compartment targeted if you choose second-class services. The thought is that thieves prefer the more affluent travellers who are in the less crowded first-class compartments.

Using a locker to store your luggage avoids the possibility of being delayed before departure in a long line at a left-luggage counter.

SIGHTSEEING
WHAT, WHEN ?

Study your guide-book and highlight important times. Museums and sites may be closed on one day of the week, free on another, or they may hike their rates during prime tourist hours.

FOR EXAMPLE:

The Taj Mahal is free on Fridays and costs only pennies other days if you go in the early morning or late after-noon. During the day the price is hiked to catch the tour groups.

The world-famous Louvre Museum in Paris is closed on Tuesdays, and cuts its general admission rate in half after 3 p.m. every other day of the week and all day on Sunday.

You can wander through both Poet's Corner and the royal chapels in London's Westminster Abbey for free if you go on a Wednesday evening.

SIGHTSEEING
WHAT, WHEN ?

"In the South
Pacific Bible
Belt...virtually
everything out-
side the churches
grinds to a halt
on Sunday. Only
hotel restaurants
will be open,
most buses and
taxis will have
vanished, and
even sports may
be banned.

"The best thing
to do on Sunday
is to go to
church...you'll
be rewarded by
the joyous
singing...you'll
encounter the
islanders on a
different level."
– David Stanley
South Pacific
Handbook
Moon Publications

Remember, in many
European and trop-
ical countries,
shops and banks
close for an hour
or two at noon.

In Israel, most
public bus ser-
vices stop for
Shabbat from late
Friday afternoon
until sunset on
Saturday.

51

SIGHTSEEING

THE GOOD NEWS

Many destinations offer interesting free opportunities:

In Austria, in the summer, numerous alpine tourist offices provide free guided hikes for visitors. In Innsbruck this has included free use of boots and a rucksack.

In France free tours are available of many wineries.

In Amsterdam and Copenhagen free tours and/or samples are sometimes available at their major breweries.

Cities such as Copenhagen have provided free bikes for sightseeing, set up in racks that can be released by making a deposit with coins.

Free "do-it-yourself" walking tour maps are available at some tourist information offices, so be sure to ask.

SIGHTSEEING

Many key museums and galleries open their doors for free one morning or evening each week. In Greece, for example, almost all museums and ancient sites are free on Sundays.

THE BAD NEWS

From popular National Parks in Ecuador and Costa Rica to the Forbidden Palace in Beijing, foreign visitors are faced with entrance rates often 10 times the amount charged to local citizens.

This can be frustrating, but remember that the local residents probably also support these facilities through their taxes.

FINDING YOUR WAY

Ask at your hotel/hostel for a brochure or letterhead with its address in the local language, or have the desk manager write it down for you. You can show it to taxi/bus drivers or pedestrians, if you lose your way.

Buy post-cards of popular sites when you arrive; you can show them to get pointed in the right direction.

If lost, head for a major hotel, department store or bank. Chances are there will be an English-speaking person on staff.

FINDING YOUR WAY

Minimize weight when sightseeing. Remove the guidebook chapter for the area you're in, staple it together and slip it into your pocket or into the back of this journal.

International fast-food chains and hotels have extra benefits. They're often your best bet for a clean Western-style toilet.

SIGHTSEEING SCAMS

There are 1,001 unexpected ways in which travellers can be separated from a little cash. Pack patience. Try, when possible, to be amused rather than angry.

On the road to Fatehpur Sikri, 40 km west of Agra, India, villagers stop tourists by blocking the road with chains. Almost everyone gets out to take a photo. Then money is demanded. Are you going to argue with a man with a bear?

In the market in Nadi, Fiji wood carvers have been known to ask a traveller for their name then quickly engrave it onto a mask. Saying no to buying the mask can lead to a nasty scene.

SIGHTSEEING SCAMS

Hiring a guide without knowing it is a situation that crops up in the Middle East, the Caribbean and South America.

A local resident will strike up a conversation about something that you're looking at. As you move along, he continues with his explanation and points out other things of interest. It's done in such a way that you feel as if you've just made a friend.

Eventually the "friend" announces that you owe a fee, which can range from reasonable to outrageous. You pay up or, again, leverage is added by creation of another nasty scene.

SIGHTSEEING STREET SAFETY

"I left my heart in Rio — and my ring, and my watch, and my camera."
— Popular T-shirt sold in Rio de Janeiro, Brazil

FREQUENTLY REPORTED PROBLEMS

Children in some European cities surround and distract a tourist by shoving paper into his/her face, while a flurry of Munchkin hands cleans out the victim's pockets.

Motorcycling teams out to rob tourists look for easy victims, with items within reach, i.e. tourists on sidewalks with their bag slung over one shoulder on the same side as the traffic, or tourists in taxis with their valuables on their laps while sitting beside an open window.

SIGHTSEEING STREET SAFETY

"The tour bus driver dropped us at the perfect spot for a shot of the Eiffel Tower. In less than a minute my friend's pack was gone. He'd just set it down for a second while he concentrated on taking a photo."
— Lucy Izon

Bag-grabbers wait where tourists stop to take photos of famous sights. Distracted travellers peering through viewfinders make easy victims in these crowded areas.

If robbed, report it to the police so that you have offical documentation for insurance.

SIGHTSEEING

STREET SAFETY

"I was in Nairobi, walking to the train station when I felt my ear being pinched. A child was behind me with one of my earrings in his hand and his eyes on the other one...don't wear anything that is a sign of wealth."
– Beth Gerstenberger Toronto, Canada

In a high-risk area where it's not necessary to carry your identification, leave your valuables and passport in the hotel safe and carry photocopies of your documentation, a small amount of cash and the name of your hotel.

In areas where cameras are popular targets, consider locking your expensive one up and carrying a disposable paper one.

SIGHTSEEING

Some travellers carry a dummy wallet with a small amount of "mugging money" that would appease a thief should they find themselves confronted and threatened.

Paris, France - "I had my coat on the back of a chair in a cafe. There was another chair behind, right up against mine. It made it easy for the person to get into my coat without my noticing."
– Josef Zankowicz Toronto, Canada

SIGHTSEEING

LOCAL TOURS

"When travelling in Nepal, if you are going to get a local guide to assist you in trekking...
make sure that the person you hire is from a reputable trekking agency and not just someone off the street. There are so many horror stories of people who have gotten burned by locals posing as trekking guides."
<u>- Larry McLaughlin</u>
<u>Edmonton, Alberta</u>

Don't head off into a remote area (e.g., a jungle trek) with a local guide or tour company that is not well known and respected by the local community and tourist board. You'll be putting yourself in a very vulnerable situation.

Ask other travellers for first-hand recommendations.

Often foreign student/youth travel agencies are good sources of information.

SIGHTSEEING

In countries such as Egypt, India and Turkey it can be cheaper for a small group to hire their own taxi to reach key sites rather than climbing on a big bus. You also have more control over how your time is spent.

"Ask another tourist right on the spot. Did you take a tour? Which company? Did they have to sit around drinking tea for two hours while one person bought a rug?... If there are three or four of you, find out what a taxi driver would charge for the same trip. The price might actually be less expensive. You'll miss out on the commentary, but you may also miss out on a two-hour shop stop and another hour lost while you circle in city traffic to pick up or drop off passengers."
- Tom Brosnahan
Turkey - A Travel
Survival Kit
Lonely Planet

STUDENT/YOUTH DISCOUNTS

Always show your student/
youth identity card and inquire before paying entrance fees, even if discounts are not posted.

WHERE TO CHECK

Transportation Services
Budget Hotels
Museums
Galleries
Parks
Tourist Sites
Restaurants
Theatres
Tour Operators

Youth Card holders are sometimes given the same discounts as students so show yours where student discounts are offered.

STUDENT/YOUTH DISCOUNTS

Travel agencies affiliated with international student and youth identity cards are often good places to check for information on local discounts. Some, such as Ireland and Canada, produce free listings.

Your youth hostel membership card may also be recognized for discounts on travel services, so always ask. In, Quito, Ecuador, for example, the Hostelling International youth hostel produces a free booklet outlining discounts around the city.

CURRENCY EXCHANGE

Have your passport handy when cashing travellers' cheques. In some countries it's even required to exchange cash.

Watch for companies that try to draw you in by offering a low exchange rate and then hit you with an exorbitant service charge.

Don't accept torn and tattered banknotes; you may have a problem spending them.

"Five of us picked up our baggage at Copenhagen's airport and got into a nearby line to exchange some money. We were shocked when we looked at our receipts; each person exchanged about $25 and was charged a $5 service fee. If we had pooled our money and sent one person to the counter we would have saved a total of $20."
— Lucy Izon

CURRENCY EXCHANGE

Because of different buying and selling rates, every time you switch currencies you lose a little, so try not to exchange any more than you will need in any one currency.

CURRENCY EXCHANGE

For a small amount of cash you may get a better deal by withdrawing what you need at an ATM with a credit card rather than paying the service charge to exchange a traveller's cheque. Credit card companies get a better rate because they exchange in bulk once a day. Service charges and interest are, however, charged from the date of the transaction.

Always try to carry some small change. Vendors cannot always make change, and in some countries it's handy for tipping in advance (a gift or a bribe depending on your viewpoint). It could make the difference between getting a seat on a bus, or a behind-the-scenes tour at an Egyptian temple.

CURRENCY EXCHANGE

Blackmarket exchange rates may be attractive but not only are the transactions illegal, travellers have also been tricked with counterfeit or out of circulation money underneath real bills.

Be wary of being diverted into a side street for a transaction. You could be being set up for a mugging.

CURIOUS CURRENCIES:

In the Cook Islands you can still find a $3 bill, and a $2 coin that is triangular in shape.

One of the problems with the 50-franc note issued in France in 1994 is that it shrinks when wet.

MONEY MATTERS
- SAFETY

Carry money and valuable documents in a pouch under your clothing. You'll be at less risk when being bumped in crowds or napping on trains and buses.

Razoring shoulder bags, day packs, fanny packs and bulging hip pockets is a favorite tactic by thieves. In really crowded areas, such as packed markets, consider wearing your daypack on your chest where you're better able to protect it.

MONEY MATTERS - SAFETY

Keep a small amount of cash accessible so you can pay for small items without having to expose the bulk of your valuables.

Couples should consider splitting their resources so that if one is robbed, the other will have enough for both to carry on until refunds are arranged.

SHOPPING

BE AWARE OF:

Bad lighting. Take a close look at the quality of items in a well-lit area before you buy.

Drivers and guides who pressure you to buy at specific shops. Your price may be inflated to cover their commission.

Torn or damaged bills as change. You may have trouble spending them, and have to waste time trying to exchange them at a bank.

Your credit card being removed from your sight. Extra slips can be engraved, and the wrong card can be returned to you.

Drinking tea with merchants can be a fun part of the shopping ritual. However, be aware that there have been rare reports of travellers feeling that their tea was spiked to lower their sales resistance.

SHOPPING

CREDIT CARD CONCERNS:

Make sure the currency is indicated beside the amount before you sign the credit card slip.

If a carbon is made of a credit card slip, request it with your receipt and destroy it.

If you are having something mailed by a vendor, paying by credit card helps to establish a paper trail if problems arise.

Save your receipts in case a customs officer challenges you on the value of your purchases when you return home.

HAGGLING

You may encounter "flexible" prices when buying a sweater in Florence, pottery in Lisbon, a carpet in Istanbul, a straw hat in Jamaica, a taxi ride in Egypt or a stereo in a duty-free shop in Fiji.

Haggling can be fun for shoppers with confidence, but for novices it can be intimidating. Here's how to increase your chances of getting a fair deal:

Research, ask other tourists what they paid for items you think you'll be shopping for.

Decide what an item is worth to you and set that as your limit.

Start by offering 50% or less of what you hope to have to pay.

If you can't agree on a sale price, try walking away. The vendor may follow you and accept your final offer.

HAGGLING

Don't make an offer you don't intend to keep; this can lead to a very ugly scene if the vendor agrees to your offer and then you decide not to buy.

Market vendors tend to haggle with cash sales in mind. If you agree on a price then pull out a credit card they may insist that you pay more because of the percentage they have to pay the credit card company.

"Use some discretion when going to the bone on a price. There's a fine line between bargaining and niggling - getting hot under the collar over 5 Baht makes both seller and buyer lose face."
- Joe Cummings
Thailand - Travel
Survival Kit
Lonely Planet

VAT

In some countries foreign visitors are eligible for a refund on a 6-20% Value Added Tax (VAT) that's added to purchases and services. Tourist information offices can explain refund availabilities and procedures, so you can determine if it will be worth the time and trouble.

You may find that only purchases made in certain stores, or for a minimum amount, are eligible for a tax refund.

You'll likely need to have your purchases, receipts and VAT forms in your carry-on luggage, available for inspection at your departure point.

Refunds given at airports may be in the local currency. You'll have to spend it before you depart or lose a chunk on a service charge to exchange it.

VAT

Refunds mailed
home may also be
in a foreign
currency. Again,
you'll lose on
service charges
to exchange the
money.

If you can get
a VAT refund
credited to your
charge card,
you could avoid
currency exchange
service charges.

In Israel,
tourists are not
charged VAT on
accommodation,
guided tours,
domestic flights
or car rentals -
if they pay in
cash.

77

SCAMS

Being aware of popular tourist scams is your best defence. Here are some familiar ones to watch out for.

Some unscrupulous jewellers in Asia (i.e. Bangkok and Jaipur) convince naive travellers that they can resell gems at home for huge profits. They'll even offer to provide names of potential buyers.

Occasionally vendors who offer to ship purchases home for travellers have switched them for items of less value. I'd take a photo of my purchase, and use a credit card to create a paper trail.

SCAMS

In Southeast Asia travellers report that they've been quoted one cover price to enter a night club then, when inside, a much higher one is demanded. Or, they were presented with an outrageously high drinks bill. Intimidation tactics are used to convince the traveller to pay up. Get trustworthy recommendations for nightclubs, and if you do get taken, report it to the police.

Beware of purchasing a cheap airline ticket with someone else's name on it. It isn't going to do you much good if the airline refuses to give you a boarding pass because the ticket name doesn't match your I.D.

ENVIRONMENTAL IMPACT

"I don't think you should give children anything — no pencils, no note-books, nothing — because it teaches them to beg. It is OK, however, to let them carry your shoulder bag or fetch some plastic water bottles or clean your boots because that demonstrates to them that they can earn decent money from honest work.

"Begging creates an endless cycle of dependence, diminishes self-worth, does more harm than good."
– Bill Dalton, Indonesia Handbook Moon Publications

ENVIRONMENTAL IMPACT

"So many travellers haven't grasped the cycle of events that they set in motion. They stay in a small lodge in Nepal, they're tired and hungry and they see a menu that has all these wonderful things on it. They order to their heart's content...they haven't considered that only one thing at a time can be cooked on the fire. There is little wood and the people are destroying what they have to give travellers what they want. Why not order the same thing, so it can be cooked at once."
– Tony Wheeler
Author/Publisher
Lonely Planet
Guidebooks

EATING ECONOMICALLY

DIFFERENT CUSTOMS

Don't assume that bread placed on your table is included in the cost of your meal. In some southern European countries, for example, you'll be charged extra for the pieces you eat.

In Australia some restaurants add surcharges on weekends and holidays, and some restaurants allow you to bring your own wine or beer.

The same cup of coffee can have three different prices in a French cafe depending on whether you sit, stand at the bar or choose a seat on the sidewalk.

In Lithuania the prices on the menu may refer to units of weight for food portions.

WHERE TO EAT CHEAP

Watch for where the local residents go; chances are they know the best value.

EATING ECONOMICALLY

Try university areas and university cafeterias (you may need a student identity card).

Some urban youth hostels have economical restaurants that even non-guests can use.

Big department stores often offer economical cafeterias.

CREDIT CARD WARNING!

Some waiters leave the tip area blank and the bill un-totalled, even when a service charge has been added, you'll not notice and tip again.

Make sure the currency is written beside the amount.

EATING ECONOMICALLY

"Sometimes, when you're feeling a little homesick, a Western fast-food restaurant is a pretty welcome sight. In Beijing my Chinese friend took me to their first Kentucky Fried Chicken outlet, where, she exclaimed with much pride, we would have 'fried chicken and smashed potatoes'."
– Lucy Izon

Check the tipping situation with a local resident before you head out to eat. In Japan and Australia, for example, tips are not expected. In France a service charge may automatically be added to your bill.

EATING ECONOMICALLY

PACK PICNICS:

If you don't have a corkscrew and can't open a bottle of wine, try loosening the cork by holding the neck of the bottle under hot water.

You can store small amounts of condiments for making sandwiches in clean film canisters.

If your pocket knife blade or utensils have gotten rusty try wiping them with raw onion.

When sitting in a restaurant or outdoor cafe, don't hang your pack on the back of your chair where it can be grabbed. Secure the strap either around your leg or the leg of your chair.

ECONOMICAL ENTERTAINMENT

Ask about special events at tourist information offices. Often, they provide a forum for free entertainment and an atmosphere that you'll never forget.

"One of the most memorable week-ends I've ever spent was at the Cattleman's Roundup in central Tasmania. From sheep dog trials to a barn dance. Everyone camped. It rained. It was great anyway."
— Lucy Izon

Western films may be presented with their original English-language soundtrack and foreign subtitles. Ask. In some countries you may be able to enjoy a popular film for a fraction of the price you would be charged at home.

ECONOMICAL ENTERTAINMENT

In London, first-run feature films are half-price on Mondays and early on Tuesdays. In Tokyo, movie tickets are usually half-price on the first day of September, December, March and June. Ask if there are days with special rates.

Economical stand-by tickets or special student rates may be available for live theatrical productions shortly before the curtain rises. Ask.

Looking for nightlife, find out where the university is and check the surrounding area.

CULTURAL CUSTOMS

Some provide
a pleasant
surprise:

In New Zealand
tea-making equip-
ment is standard
in most hotel and
motel rooms.

Some differences
you'll find amus-
ing:

In Iceland every-
one is listed by
their first name
in the telephone
book.

Read up on local
customs before
you go so you
don't innocently
cause offence or
wind up in seri-
ous trouble.

Blowing your nose
in public in
Japan, expressing
affection openly
in China, picking
up food with your
left hand in
Indonesia, touch-
ing a friend on
the head in
Thailand or
allowing the
soles of your
feet to point in
their direction,
all can cause
great discomfort
to local
residents.

CULTURAL CUSTOMS

In Singapore, chewing gum or spitting can earn you a hefty fine.

In some countries, such as in the Czech and Slovakian Republics, foreign visitors not staying in hotels must register with the local police.

To demonstrate disrespect towards the Thai Royal family can be a criminal offence

Check your guidebook for advice on how to dress for the area you are in. You may not agree with the customs, but ignoring them may earn you an uncomfortable amount of attention, and you may be turned away at tourist sites.

HEALTH - SEEKING HELP

"I arrived in Athens suffering from a painful infection on a Sunday. I found an advertisement for an English-speaking doctor who was open. For the three minutes I spent with him he wanted $80 US cash. I suspect it was a special inflated rate for tourists."
– Lucy Izon

Well-researched guidebooks should include informa-tion on emergency services, and embassies and consulates should be able to pro-vide the names of doctors used by their staff and other travellers.

HEALTH - SEEKING HELP

If you find your-self in a situation where it's necessary to have an injection by syringe, make sure you see it being removed from a sealed package so you know it's new and sterile.

If you decide to go the herbal medication route, remember that although it's natural, it's not risk-free. Some herbal remedies are just as pow-erful as drugs and can interact with other medications.

HEALTH -
TREATMENT
WARNINGS

"I'd be careful
if it's an expen-
sive drug and
they're selling
it to you really,
really cheaply—
that's a bad
sign."
- Philip
Scappatura M.D.

Some pharmaceuti-
cals are fakes.
In Cambodia cap-
sules containing
mixtures of sugar
and flour have
been sold as
antibiotics. In
other areas of
Southeast Asia
chalk and talcum
powder have been
repackaged con-
vincingly as
medicine.

Try to buy from a
pharmacy attached
to a hospital, or
from one known
and used by the
staff of your
embassy.

You could be at
risk for serious
diseases, such as
Hepatitis B or
HIV, if proper
precautions have
not been taken
when needles are
used for:

dental work

tattooing

body and ear
piercing

HEALTH - TREATMENT WARNINGS

acupuncture

vaccinations

blood transfu-
sions

Being cut with a
contaminated
instrument such
as a shared razor
can also be
risky. Think
twice before you
settle in for a
quick shave at a
street stall in
India.

"One morning in
Mexico I looked
in my mirror and
my mouth was com-
pletely black. I
thought I had
some kind of
plague!
Eventually I
found the packag-
ing for some
Pepto-Bismol I'd
taken the night
before. There, in
very fine print
it warned: May
cause temporary
darkening of
tongue. Next time
I'll read the
fine print
first."
– Lucy Izon

POPULAR FOLK MEDICINE

TREATMENTS FOR COLDS:

Stuffed up? Drape your head with a towel, carefully lean over a bowl of steaming water and breathe in the trapped moist air.

Eating hot, spicy foods can also help clear the air passages.

Mustard, garlic, onions and ginger are all popular natural treatments, along with the age-old remedy - sipping chicken soup.

WHAT TO AVOID

Milk

Don't over-use your decongestant. Too much nasal spray can have a rebound effect and cause swelling of the nasal passages. Read the packaging.

POPULAR FOLK MEDICINE

TO SOOTHE A SORE THROAT:

Try tea with honey, or gargle with warm water that has a tea-spoon of salt dissolved in it.

Make yourself a hot-water bottle by filling a plastic twist-top soda bottle with hot water. Seal it in a plastic bag, then wrap it in a towel or slip it into a large sock.

TOOTHACHES

For pain relief
until you can get
to a dentist,
try:

an ice pack
wrapped in a
towel held
against your face

ice on the web of
skin between
your thumb and
first finger,
especially on the
same side as the
pain

swishing some
warm salty water
or whiskey in
your mouth

a dab of oil of
clove on some
cotton wool,
placed directly
on the tooth, not
the gum

* Don't put ASA
(aspirin) on your
gum.

TOOTHACHES

If you need to go for dental work, especially in the Third World, ask your embassy or consulate for a recommendation. Not only do you have to be careful about sterile equipment, you also want to be sure that the water pumped into your mouth isn't going to cause you problems.

HEALTH - FOOD & DRINK PRECAUTIONS

The general rule for Third World countries is: if you can't peel it, cook it or boil it, don't eat it.

Clean your hands before touching anything you're going to eat.

Look for cooked foods that have just been pre-pared.

Watch out for fresh vegtables and fruit that have been rinsed in tainted water.

If you can't drink the water, don't expect the ice cubes to be any safer.

Check that the seal is intact on any bottled water you're served. Bottles are some-times refilled from taps and resold.

HEALTH - FOOD & DRINK PRECAUTIONS

If you have a choice, go with bottled carbonated rather than still water.

If you don't like the carbonation, pass the liquid between two glasses several times and the bubbles will be reduced. This works with any carbonated drink.

Soft drinks should be opened in front of you so you know that they haven't been diluted with local water.

Carry your own small water bottle, so you can use it rather than tap water to brush your teeth.

In the Orient consider carrying your own chop-sticks so you can be sure of their condition.

HEALTH - TOURISTA

Montezuma's revenge, the Pharaoh's curse, Delhi belly, Tourista, what ever you want to call it, being on the road with the runs is a lousy experience.

Two ways to decrease your chance of having problems:

Wash your hands before you pick up anything to put it in your mouth.

Eat yogurt. It contains lacto-bacillus, a bacterial culture which can inhibit the bacteria that cause Tourista. Try "safe" or pre-packaged yogurt as both a prevention and a treatment.

If you succumb:

Drink fluids to avoid dehydra-tion: tea, bottled water, chicken noodle soup and soft drinks. Nibble on saltine crackers. Stay away from too much sugar or sodium.

HEALTH - TOURISTA

Rehydration solutions are available at drugstores and pharmacies.

Avoid:
dairy products
alcohol
high-fibre foods
fatty foods
caffeine

Stick With:
bananas
potatoes
noodles
apple sauce
plain toast
carrot soup

Drinking tea or curling up with a hot water bottle may help relieve muscle spasms.

HEALTH - FEET

You can reduce the friction that causes blisters when you wear new or wet footwear by applying Vaseline or powder to your feet. Add mole-skin to tender spots before trouble develops.

Wear cheap plastic sandals when using shared showers to pro-tect yourself from athlete's foot.

If you have a problem, try to keep your feet clean and dry.

Folk treatments include:

soaking your feet in warm water with black tea bags

applying a paste of baking soda and water.

HEALTH - FEET

Check boots
stored outside
overnight for
snakes, spiders,
etc.

Leaky boots? Slip
plastic bags over
your socks. Your
feet may still
get damp from
perspiration but
it'll be more
comfortable than
freezing water.

Opt for wool
socks. Wool
retains heat
when wet.

Stuff wet boots
with newspaper
and sit near a
heat source to
speed up the dry-
ing process.

Don't put leather
too close to
direct heat — it
will warp.

If you're having
a problem with
laces that keep
coming loose,
dampen them
before you tie
them.

BEAT THE HEAT

"I believe that in India 'cold weather' is merely a conventional phrase and has come into use through the necessity of having some way to distinguish between weather which will melt a brass door-knob and weather which will only make it mushy."
— Mark Twain

It can take several weeks for your body to adapt to a hot climate.

Wear lightweight and light-colored, loose-fitting clothing. Cotton is the most comfortable.

Just drinking enough fluids to quench your thirst is not necessarily enough to keep you healthy. Dark urine, or lack of urine, are signs of dehydration. This can lead to a painful internal infection, especially for women.

BEAT THE HEAT

A dampened cloth around your neck will not only protect a tender area from the sun, but also help you feel cooler.

At hotels in Asia it is sometimes possible to get a day pass to the pool for a small fee. Try asking.

If you have your travellers' cheques and passport in a cotton money belt/pouch, wrap them in plastic so signatures are not spoiled by perspiration.

SIZZLING SUNBURN

You may be at greater risk than you realize. Medications that can increase your skin's sensitivity to ultraviolet light include:

antibiotics

some antimalarials

antifungal medications

antihistamines

diuretics

drugs for diabetes

oral contraceptives

tranquillizers

* Don't forget you can burn even if it's foggy or cloudy, and it's easier to burn at higher altitudes.

* Wear a t-shirt when snorkeling to protect your back and shoulders.

SOOTHING THE SIZZLE:

Drink plenty of water to avoid dehydration.

SIZZLING SUNBURN

Folk remedies for relief include:

Applying aloe vera on skin.

A paste of cool plain yogurt on skin, rinsed off with cool water after half an hour.

Treating eyes by covering lids with cucumber slices, or tea bags squeezed in cool water.

Anti-inflammatories may provide relief, but young travellers should be aware that ASA (aspirin) has been associated with the potentially fatal Reye's syndrome in teenagers and children.

If you can't sleep because rubbing against sheets with sunburned skin is painful, spreading some powder on the sheets may help reduce the friction.

BORDERS

Some borders you'll sail through, at others, you'll have to accept being interrogated. Have patience. Remember, nobody has to let you in. And remember it's your responsibility to know the entry requirements to the country you're visiting.

Don't dress in the "destitute" look; you may be considered a potential burden.

You may need to show that:

Your passport will be valid for up to six months after entry.

You have sufficient funds for your visit.

You have a ticket to leave.

Make sure that you've had all required inoculations. You don't want to have to get shots at the last minute at a facility you don't trust.

BORDERS

Dual Citizenship:

Through birth, marriage or naturalization you may be regarded by another country to be one of its citizens. If so, after entering you could be subject to special taxes or military duty. Be sure to check in advance.

Overstaying your visa's validity in countries such as Indonesia can lead to a jail sentence.

When entering countries (such as Israel) whose stamp in your passport could restrict you from travel to some other areas, you can request a temporary stamp on a sheet of paper that will be removed when you leave.

DRUGS

"While travelling from Singapore to Thailand, a Thai on our bus asked a Swede to wear his new boots, because he was over his duty limit. We couldn't believe the Swede agreed to do this for a stranger. Right at the border there was a sign saying the death penalty was imposed for drug smuggling."
- Pat Raes
Toronto, Canada

Don't carry parcels or clothing across a border for anyone.

Be cautious about crossing borders in someone else's vehicle. If they are carrying something illegal, you could be in serious trouble just through association.

You will be subject to the laws of the country you are entering. Some foreign legal systems view detainees as guilty until proven innocent.

DRUGS

Keep an eye on your luggage before border crossings. Secure it so nothing can be slipped into it.

Don't let the fact that drugs are readily available and commonly used in some foreign countries mislead you into thinking that authorities will not arrest offenders. In some cases the very people who sell them also tip off the police for rewards.

In 1994, a 20-year-old Toronto woman was caught trying to smuggle drugs out of Jamaica. Police believed she was a "patsy" - set up by a gang to get caught, in the hopes that customs officers would then relax and other carriers could manage to slide through.

PHONING HOME

"I was in Bangalore, India and trying to be thrifty, but rather than go out to find a telephone at night I made a 7-minute call home from my room. The next day I was presented with a bill for more than $100 U.S. The hotel had slapped on a $70 service charge. Later I visited an orphanage. I was able to buy lunch for 400 kids for $18. That phone call could have fed those 400 children more than five meals."
– Debra Cummings
Travel Editor
Calgary Herald

Never assume that because you are using a direct dial operator or a calling card that a hotel won't try to gouge you with surcharges.

Some hotels will even charge you if your party does not answer after a minimum amount of time.

PHONING HOME

Post offices are often the best places for economical overseas calls and fax services.

Consider the Internet as an alternative.

"I've just returned from two weeks in Nepal. If anyone is going there and wants to contact home, you might want to try ATM-Telelinks in Kathmandu. You can send a 1k message to any Internet address for 75 Rs."
– Larry McLaughlin
Edmonton, Alberta

Watch out for surfers - not on the net, but the ones lurking near your phone booth. Rail and bus stations are ideal areas for thieves who watch for tourists using calling cards. They note the number keyed in and immediately resell that information for illegal use.

MAIL

Ask those sending you mail to print and underline your last name.

If you are receiving your mail c/o Poste Restante (General Delivery) it's likely to be at the central post office. You may have to pay a small fee, and you may need identification to collect it.

Missing mail may be misfiled. Check under:

The initial for your first name.

M for Mr., Ms., or Miss.

Similar-looking initials, such as an N for M, or an I for an L.

In some countries the contents of a parcel will have to be inspected before it's mailed. Check before wrapping and sealing.

In China, wrapping paper, string, etc., are sold at post offices. Put the address inside in case of damage.

MAIL

Paper bags can double as wrapping paper.

Stamps can, and have been (in India), removed from mail. Take your parcel to the post office and see that the stamps are canceled so that they have no value if removed.

You may save time by sending from the central post office in a large city.

If you agree to let a shopkeeper package and mail a purchase for you, you run the risk of the item being switched for something of less value, or of the item not being sent at all. If you decide to do this, try to pay with a credit card so you'll have a trail back to them if you're not satisfied.

Cover the writing on post-cards and parcels with clear tape to protect from damage by dampness.

PHOTOGRAPHY - GENERAL

Photographing foreign police, military, airports, rail stations or customs areas may be an offence, depending on the country you are visiting. If in doubt, ask. You could lose your film or be detained.

You can get an idea of interesting subjects to photograph by looking at local postcards. Work on finding your own special view. Try to tell a story with your photo.

When shooting scenery, see if you can position something (such as a road) in the foreground to lead your eye into the shot. Try to keep the horizon or the object you are focusing on a third of the way from the edge of the photograph, rather than in the dead centre, so the finished shot isn't divided in half.

PHOTOGRAPHY - GENERAL

Bright mid-day sun is harsh. It's the soft light of early morning or warm glow that appears late in the afternoon that is most complementary to faces and scenery.

A trick for judging the amount of time to sunset is to extend your hand toward the hori- zon and count the number of fingers you can fit between the ground and the sun. For each finger you'll have approximate- ly 10 minutes.

Make sure your name and address is inside your camera case, and on your camera if possible.

PHOTOGRAPHY TIPS

Avoid condensation. Don't ever leave your camera sitting on an air-conditioning unit.

Most museums restrict the use of flashes. Some won't let you take photographs at all. Go prepared with fast speed film - at least 400 ASA.

Use a polarizing filter and shoot at a 35 degree angle to reduce reflection on windows and glass cases.

"The mistake I make the most is not getting close enough to my subject. Filling the frame is more dramatic. When I think I've got a good shot I have to remember to move a little closer."
– Lucy Izon

PHOTOGRAPHY TIPS

For scenic shots (such as mountain views) try to put a person in the foreground to provide perspective on size.

Sparkling white sand on a beach can fool an automatic camera. Check setting suggestions in your film box, and try shots using the plus one (+1) feature.

In desert areas keep your camera in a sealed plastic bag to shield it from dust. Protect the camera and your film from intense heat.

COLD WEATHER PHOTOGRAPHY

Electronic cameras and camera batteries can stop working in very cold weather. Keep your camera warm and carry spare batteries in a pocket where they'll receive heat from your body, and rotate them when needed.

Oils can interfere with battery connections - handle with clean hands.

In winter weather put your camera inside a sealed plastic bag before you bring it inside, so that condensation forms on the bag, not in your camera.

Don't manually rewind film quickly in very cold weather. The film can become brittle and snap, or you could cause static electricity, which shows on your photographs.

COLD WEATHER PHOTOGRAPHY

Snow is highly reflective and can fool your camera into taking under-exposed photographs:

Check the setting sugges-tions indicated in the box in which your film is packaged.

In bright condi-tions, if your camera automati-cally sets the film speed, try shots using the +1 exposure setting.

If the speed of the film you're using must be set manually on your camera, set the dial to one-half of the film's actual speed. Reset when light conditions change.

PHOTOGRAPHING PEOPLE

"I focused my telephoto lens on two elderly men surrounded by a display of bright red fireworks. Suddenly, a tiny woman in a flowing brown robe tore across the temple square, planted herself six inches from my nose and screamed at me. A crowd gathered. I had no idea what was going on.

"My Chinese friend explained. The woman thought I'd taken her photograph, something that for her was deeply disturbing. Fortunately, by listening calmly until her anger was spent I was able to retreat, camera and film intact."
– Lucy Izon

Respect your subjects, not all will want to be photographed. How you treat them will redound on future travellers who pass the same way. Consider how you'd feel if this happened to you at home.

PHOTOGRAPHING PEOPLE

People are often more willing to let you photograph them if you take time to communicate with them before pointing your camera.

Remove any sunglasses, show your camera, smile and wait for their response.

Some people will want to be paid. If you're uncomfortable with this, consider a small gift (food?) as a gesture of goodwill, or, if it's a vendor buy a small item.

PHOTOGRAPHING PEOPLE

Try for eye contact. Set up your shot and just before you take it, attract your subject's attention.

When photographing children, get down to their eye level. Something to fascinate them (such as liquid blowing bubbles) can lead to delightful facial expressions.

Pay attention to your background. Watch for ugly electrical wires, or telephone poles that seem to sprout out of a subject's head.

Watch for shadows on your subjects, or subjects who are squinting into the sun.

PHOTOGRAPHING PEOPLE

"Red eye" appears when your camera captures the blood vessels in your subjects' dilated eyes. Some new cameras have features to reduce red eye. If yours doesn't, try this:

If you're able, tilt your flash up to bounce light off the ceiling.

Increase the light in the room so pupils will decrease in size.

Avoid having the subjects look directly at the camera.

Adjust to a wide angle.

Take two flash shots in a row. Pupils should be reduced for the second.

WET WEATHER PHOTOGRAPHY

Overcast weather can be flattering to some subjects, such as flowers, whose colors will usually appear very rich.

Adding brightly colored items such as a yellow poncho or red daypack to a drizzling setting can create a much more appealing photograph.

Protect your camera from rain by wrapping it in a plastic bag secured around the lens with a rubber band. Leave enough over the lens to create a protective hood.

Or, pack it and use a cheap paper one for the day.

"I wrap my camera in a t-shirt, before putting it in my pack, to protect it from condensation."
– Dr. Kay Kepler
Ecologist/Author

WET WEATHER PHOTOGRAPHY

You can compensate for reduced daylight by using a faster speed film. The trade-off will be a slightly grainier photograph.

If you don't have a fast-speed film (e.g., 400 ASA) you can "push" the film speed on manual cameras. Set the higher speed, shoot the entire roll, mark it and take it to a professional developer.

Saltwater spray can be corrosive and damage your camera.

Heading for a high-humidity location? Slip a silica-gel packet into your camera bag. They are provided free in shoe boxes when you buy leather products.

PHOTOGRAPHY - FILM

The faster the speed of your film, the more sensitive it is to light and damage by airport X-ray machines.

Have all your films in hand, in a clear plastic bag. The easier you make it for security staff to hand inspect your film the less chance they'll insist on putting it through an X-ray machine.

Before buying film, check the expiration date, and never buy at a tourist site where it's been sitting exposed to heat.

PHOTOGRAPHY - FILM

Before having all your films processed in a foreign destination, do a test roll.

Empty film canisters can be recycled as waterproof containers to hold a mending kit, jewelry, extra camera batteries, stamps, condiments, or small amounts of suntan lotion, ointment or toothpaste.

If you use daylight film indoors, the red and warm colors in your photo will be exaggerated. If you use indoor film outside, the cool blue colors will be stronger.

LAUNDRY

"At the youth hostel in Quito, Ecuador, there is a laundromat adjoining the main building for guests and the public. It's an ideal place to meet local residents."
– Lucy Izon

Where to look for reasonably priced "do-it-yourself" facilities:

Youth hostels, but they may limit use to their own guests.

Near student residences.

Campgrounds.

If your sink plug is missing, try choking the entry to the drain with a plastic bag, or lining the sink with a large garbage bag or plastic poncho.

Hot water can set some stains. For blood or chocolate try rubbing with soap and washing in cold water.

LAUNDRY

Salt or soda water can help remove wine stains.

Liberally sprinkle powder onto grease stains to absorb oil before cleaning. Then rub in detergent and wash in very hot water.

Help your clothes to dry quickly by first wrapping them in a towel to absorb excess moisture.

Don't dry clothes on stained wooden furniture or hangers. The dye can transfer to the cloth.

If you have to repack damp clothes, put them in a resealable plastic bag.

Hanging clothes in a steaming bathroom will help to remove wrinkles.

CREEPING CRITTERS

"I've had dengue...if you've been in an area where there are mosquitoes and a week later your brain feels like it's being fried in oil while a red hot poker with big hooks on the end runs down your back, and the hooks are in your gut, well welcome to the club..."
– Lynn Williams
Key West, Florida

Malaria, dengue, yellow fever and encephalitis are a few of the diseases transmitted by insects. Your best defence is not getting bitten in the first place.

Don't bank on budget tour companies providing bed nets. Be prepared with your own.

CREEPING CRITTERS

Check your net
for tiny tears.
Sew, twist and
pin, or block
them with tape on
both sides.

Position your net
so you won't lie
against it in
your sleep.

ITEMS THAT MAY ATTRACT INSECTS:

scented shampoos,
deodorants, soaps
and suntan lotion

perspiration

dark colors

bright colors

TO DISCOURAGE INSECTS:

wear light or
khaki colors, and
stick with long
sleeves and pants
in high-risk
situations.

CREEPING CRITTERS

"Deet" is considered by many experts to be the most successful compound contained in insect repellents. Don't use it on broken skin or around your eyes, keep it off nylon and plastics (e.g., your glasses).

To reduce itching from bites try:

washing with soap and water

applying a paste of baking soda and water

a dab of tooth-paste

ice

Anti-inflamatory or allergy med-ication may also help.

CREEPING CRITTERS

Australians discourage flies around their faces by hanging corks from the brim of their hats.

If critters crawl out of your drain at night when the lights are off, spread moth balls around the hole. Your hostel/hotel manager may have some.

MEET THE PEOPLE

Collect all contact names you are offered by family, friends or people you meet during your journey. A few hours in a foreign home could be one of your most memorable experiences.

Japan, Israel, Brussels, Denmark, Jamaica, India, and the Bahamas have all offered free "Meet the People" programs, enabling travellers to visit with local residents and sometimes spend several hours in their home. Check details with tourist information offices.

MEET THE PEOPLE

"Equipped with hometown post-cards and pictures of my family, I make a point to give as much from my culture as I'm taking from my host's cul-ture....I insist on no special treatment, telling my host that I'm most comfortable when no fuss is made over me. I try to help with the chores, I don't wear out my welcome, and I follow up each visit with post-cards."
- Rick Steves
Europe Through the Back Door

ALTITUDE

Those who arrive quickly at high altitudes, by plane or bus, increase their risk of mountain sickness.

Ideally, hikers should plan slow ascents, with rest days, to give their bodies a chance to get acclimatized.

"It's the altitude you sleep at at night that makes the biggest difference. Because during the day, if you are getting short of breath and having problems, you breathe faster or you go to a lower altitude. If you fly up to a high altitude and go to sleep and any of those symptoms occur you don't notice. It's much more dangerous."
– Philip Scappatura MD

ALTITUDE

Sleeplessness, loss of appetite, headache, nausea, vomiting, a sense of "fullness" in the chest, drowsiness, abnormal behavior, a "drunken" walk, are all signs that can indicate mountain sickness. In extreme cases it can be fatal.

Remember that it's easier to get a sunburn at high altitudes, so put on sunblock and wear protective glasses.

The best light for photography will likely be in the early morning and late afternoon. A polarizing filter can help reduce problems with haze.

WOMEN

Trust your gut. If a hotel doesn't feel comfortable, move on. Remember, the staff have keys.

Don't open a hotel room door to just anyone who says they're staff. Call the desk and check.

Youth hostels usually offer a comfortable environment for solo women travellers. It's easy to socialize in the kitchen or common room and make friends with other travellers. Some foreign YWCAs also offer lodging in a similar environment.

Bare legs, exposed shoulders, an uncovered head and even wearing sandals can be offensive in some areas of the world, especially Muslim countries. Check your guide-book. Carry a large scarf or sarong to cover up at religious sites.

WOMEN

Holding a map and looking bewildered can attract unwanted attention. Walk with a sense of purpose, even when you're not sure.

Leave a trail, let people know where you're heading.

If you are frustrated with being stared at, don sunglasses to at least stop eye contact.

"One traveller reported that his female friend was in a shower block at a Sinai beach resort, when she turned and saw three curious young boys checking her out. From then on they kept a watch on the door of any secluded facilities."
– Lucy Izon

HEALTH -
HEADING HOME

"Twelve days after leaving the jungle on the northwest border of Thailand I was knocked down with what felt like a terrible flu. I was amazed to find out it was malaria because I was taking anti-malarial medication. I had, however, been in an area known for resistance. Knowing the symptoms and where to get specialized help may have saved my life."
– Lucy Izon

Be aware of medical risks and their symptoms in the regions where you've been travelling.

Always take the full course of your prescriptions even if you've left a risk area. The medication may be combating something already in your system.

HEALTH - HEADING HOME

Some serious tropical diseases, such as malaria, tuberculosis and bilharzia, can take weeks, months and even years to surface.

Family physicians can miss such exotic diagnoses.

If you have suspicious symptoms, tell your doctor where you've been. If the symptoms are severe, see a travel health specialist or go to a hospital that has a tropical disease unit.

If you do get medical attention abroad, try to get the hospital to itemize your bill into various services for your insurance claim.

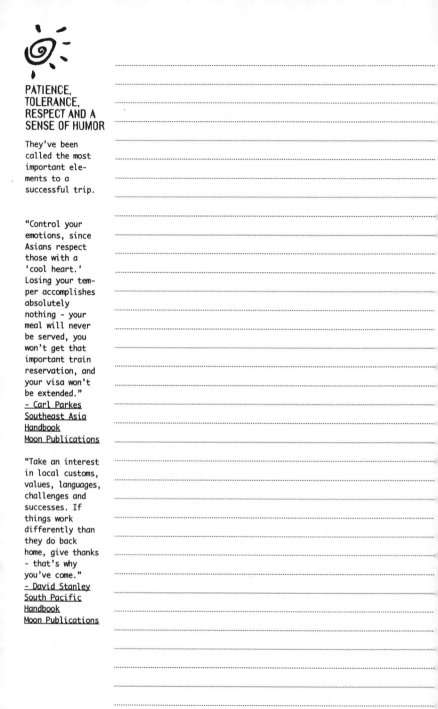

PATIENCE, TOLERANCE, RESPECT AND A SENSE OF HUMOR

They've been called the most important elements to a successful trip.

"Control your emotions, since Asians respect those with a 'cool heart.' Losing your temper accomplishes absolutely nothing - your meal will never be served, you won't get that important train reservation, and your visa won't be extended."
- Carl Parkes
Southeast Asia
Handbook
Moon Publications

"Take an interest in local customs, values, languages, challenges and successes. If things work differently than they do back home, give thanks - that's why you've come."
- David Stanley
South Pacific
Handbook
Moon Publications

PATIENCE, TOLERANCE, RESPECT AND A SENSE OF HUMOR

"I was in India and withering at the end of a long sweltering day—I just wanted a bottle of cold water. At the front desk of my hotel I was told to go to my room and it would be delivered. I didn't want room service, I just wanted water. My request fell on deaf ears. I wouldn't get the water without going to my room and paying for someone to carry it to me. Frustrated I went and waited. Twenty minutes later there was a knock at my door. There stood three men balancing a refrigerator, inside of which was my bottle of water."

– Lucy Izon

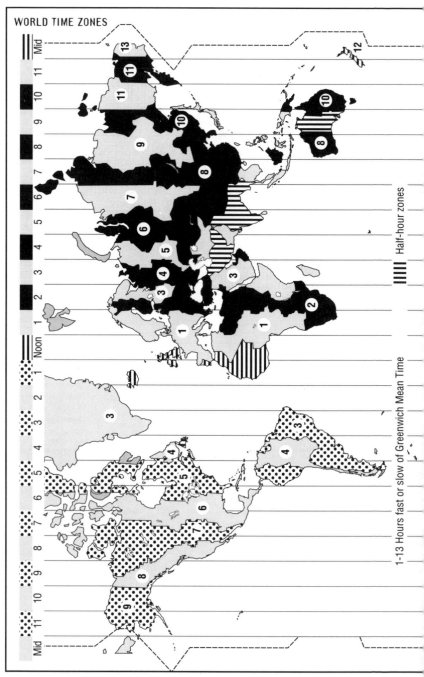

WORLD TIME ZONES

Half-hour zones

1-13 Hours fast or slow of Greenwich Mean Time

147

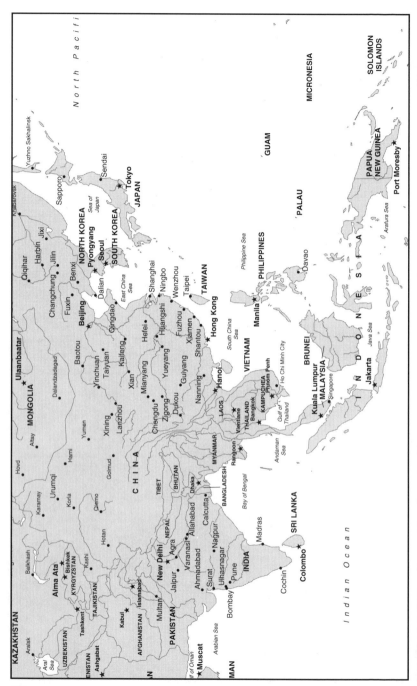

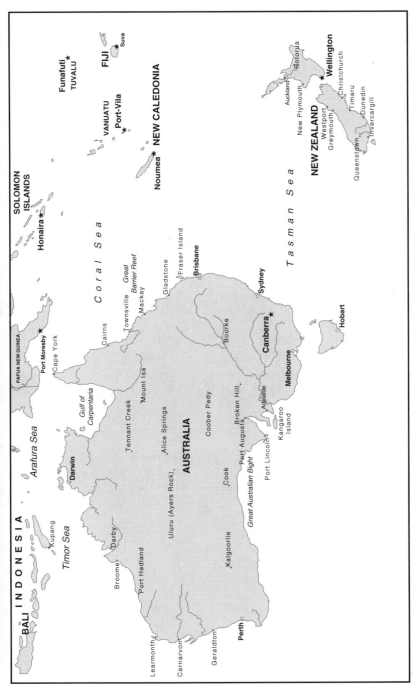

Caribbean Sea

Kingstown
Castries
St. George's

NICARAGUA
Bluefields
Managua
Barranquilla
San Jose
Panama
COSTA RICA
PANAMA

Valencia Caracas
VENEZUELA
Cucuta
Medellin
Georgetown
Paramaribo
Bogota
Puerto Ayacucho
GUYANA
Cayenne
COLOMBIA
SURINAME
FRENCH GUIANA
Boa Vista
Camopi
Pasto
Mitu
Serro Do Navio
Macapa
ECUADOR
Quito
Belem
Sao Luis
Galápagos Is.
Guayaquil
Cuenca
Manaus
Santarem
Fortaleza
Iquitos
Tefe
Talara
PERU
Sao Goncalo
Teresina
Chiclayo
Orellana
Jacareacanga
Imperatriz
Trujillo
Tarauaça
Porto Velho
Cachimbo
Recife
Huaraz
Rio Branco
Maceio
Huanuco
BRAZIL
Gurupi
Barreiras
Aracaju
Cerro De Pasco
Alvorada
Lima
Huancayo
Salvador
Ayacucho
Ica
Cuzco
BOLIVIA
Brasilia
Canavieiras
Puno
La Paz
Cuiaba
Goiania
Santa Cruz
Arica
Sucre
Belo Horizonte
Iquique
Campo Grande
Vitoria
Tarija
Boa Vista
Rio de Janeiro
PARAGUAY
Campinas
Antofagasta
Asuncion
Iguazú Falls
Sao Paulo
Salta
Curitiba
CHILE
San Miguel de Tucuman
Resistencia
Florianopolis
Porto Alegre
Cordoba
Tacuarembo
Valparaiso
Santiago
Rosario
URUGUAY
Buenos Aires
Durazno
Concepcion
ARGENTINA
Montevideo
Neuquen
Bahia Blanca
Mar del Plata
Valdivia
San Carlos de Bariloche
Puerto Montt
Rawson

Comodoro Rivadavia

Puerto Santa Cruz
FALKLAND ISLANDS
Rio Gallegos
Port Stanley
Tierra del Fuego
Ushuaia
Cape Horn

SOUTH GEORGIA ISLAND

English	French	German	Spanish	Italian	Portuguese	Japanese	Thai
1. Hello	1. Bonjour	1. Hallo	1. Hola	1. Salve/Ciao	1. Olá	1. Kon-nichiwa	1. sa wad dee krap
2. My Name is	2. Je m'appelle	2. Mein Name ist	2. Me llamo	2. Il mio nome è...	2. O meu nome é	2. Watashi wa...desu	2. phom / di-chan cheu
3. Yes	3. Oui	3. Ja	3. Sí	3. Sì	3. Sim	3. Hai	3. krap / ka
4. No	4. Non	4. Nein	4. No	4. No	4. Não	4. I-i-e	4. my krap / my ka
5. Please	5. S'il-vous-plaît	5. Bitte	5. Por favor	5. Per favore	5. Por favor	5. Doozo	5. prot / kor
6. Thank you	6. Merci	6. Danke	6. Gracias	6. Grazie	6. Obrigado	6. Arigatoo gozaimasu	6. korp koon /Korp jy
7. Where?	7. Où?	7. Wo?	7. ¿Dónde?	7. Dove?	7. Onde?	7. Doko?	7. teeny
8. Which?	8. Lequel?	8. Welche?	8. ¿Cuál?	8. Quale?	8. Qual?	8. Dole?	8. ny
9. Why?	9. Pourquoi?	9. Warum?	9. ¿Por qué?	9. Perché?	9. Porquê?	9. Naze?	9. tum my
10. When?	10. Quand?	10. Wann?	10. ¿Cuándo?	10. Quando?	10. Quando?	10. Itsu?	10. meu-a ry
11. How much?	11. Beaucoup?	11. Wieviel?	11. ¿Cuánto?	11. Quanto?	11. Quanto custa?	11. Ikura?	11. towry
12. How Many?	12. Combien?	12. Wie viele?	12. ¿Cuántos?	12. Quanti?	12. Quantos?	12. Ikutsu?	12. towry
13. Good-bye	13. Au revoir	13. Auf Wiedersehen	13. Adiós	13. Ciao	13. Adeus	13. Sayoonara	13. lah (gorn)
14. Sunday	14. Dimanche	14. Sonntag	14. Domingo	14. domenica	14. Domingo	14. Nichiyoobi	14. wun ahit
15. Monday	15. Lundi	15. Montag	15. Lunes	15. lunedì	15. Segunda-feira	15. Getsuyoobi	15. wun jun
16. Tuesday	16. Mardi	16. Dienstag	16. Martes	16. martedì	16. Terça-feira	16. Kayoobi	16. wun ungkahn
17. Wednesday	17. Mercredi	17. Mittwoch	17. Miércoles	17. mercoledì	17. Quarta-feira	17. Suiyoobi	17. wun poot
18. Thursday	18. Jeudi	18. Donnerstag	18. Jueves	18. giovedì	18. Quinta-feira	18. Mokuyoobi	18. wun pa reu hut
19. Friday	19. Vendredi	19. Freitag	19. Viernes	19. venerdì	19. Sexta-feira	19. Kin-yoobi	19. wun sook
20. Saturday	20. Samedi	20. Sonnabend/Samstag	20. Sábado	20. sabato	20. Sábado	20. Doyoobi	20. wun sow
21. Single room	21. Chambre simple	21. Einzelzimmer	21. Habitación simple	21. Camera singola	21. Quarto individual	21. Shinguru no heya	21. horng du-o
22. double room	22. Chambre double	22. Doppelzimmer	22. Habitación doble	22. Camera doppia	22. Quarto duplo	22. Daburu no heya	22. horng koo
23. dormitory bed	23. Lit de dortoir	23. Schlafsaal	23. Cama de dormitorio	23. Dormitorio	23. Cama de dormitório	23. Lyoo beddo	23. dtee-ang norm rua-m
24. 1st class	24. 1ère classe	24. Erster Klasse	24. Primera clase	24. Prima classe	24. Primeira classe	24. Ikkyuu	24. chun tee neung
25. 2nd class	25. 2ème classe	25. Zweiter Klasse	25. Segunda clase	25. Seconda classe	25. Segunda classe	25. Nikyuu	25. chun tee sorng
26. airport	26. Aéroport	26. Flughafen	26. aeropuerto	26. aeroporto	26. Aeroporto	26. Kuukoo	26. sa-nahm bin
27. allergy	27. Allergie	27. Allergie	27. alergia	27. allergia	27. Alergia	27. Alerugi-i	27. rok poom phae
28. antibiotics	28. Antibiotiques	28. Antibiotika	28. antibióticos	28. antibiotici	28. Antibióticos	28. Kooseebusshitsu	28. ya patichiwana
29. antiseptic	29. Antiseptiques	29. Desinfektionsmittel	29. antiséptico	29. antisettico	29. Desinfectante	29. Boofuzai	29. ya gun now
30. automobile	30. Automobile	30. Auto, Wagen	30. automóvil	30. automobile	30. Automóvel	30. Kuluma	30. kreu-ang yon
31. bank	31. Banque	31. Bank	31. banco	31. banca	31. Banco	31. Ginkoo	31. tanah kahn
32. beach	32. Plage	32. Strand	32. playa	32. spiaggia	32. Praia	32. Kaigan	32. chai ta lay
33. bed	33. Lit	33. Bett	33. cama	33. letto	33. Cama	33. Beddo	33. dtee-ang
34. boat	34. Bateau	34. Boot, Schiff	34. bote	34. barca	34. Barco	34. Bo-oto	34. reu-a
35. boiled	35. Bouilli	35. gekocht	35. hervido(a)	35. bollito	35. Fervido	35. Yudeta	35. dtom
36. bottle opener	36. Ouvre-bouteille	36. Flaschenöffner	36. abridor de botellas	36. apribottiglie	36. Saca-rolhas	36. Bin a-ke	36. tee pert koo-at
37. battery	37. Batterie	37. Batterie	37. pila	37. batteria	37. Bateria (automóvel)	37. Bateri-i	37. tahn fy chai
38. beer	38. Bière	38. Bier	38. cerveza	38. birra	38. Cerveja	38. Bi-iru	38. num beer
39. big/small	39. Grand / petit	39. groß / klein	39. grande/pequeño(a)	39. grande/piccolo	39. Grande/pequeno	39. O-ki-i/Chi-isai	39. yy, dto / lek
40. blanket	40. Couverture	40. Wolldecke	40. manta	40. coperta	40. Cobertor	40. Mo-ofu	40. pah horn
41. bread	41. Pain	41. Brot	41. pan	41. pane	41. Pão	41. Pan	41. kanom pung
42. breakfast	42. Petit-déjeuner	42. Frühstück	42. desayuno	42. colazione	42. Pequeno almoço	42. Cho-oshoku	42. ah hahn chow
43. broken	43. Cassé	43. gebrochen	43. roto(a)	43. rotto	43. Partido	43. Kowaleteiru	43. dtaak, huk
44. burn	44. Brûlé	44. verbrannt	44. quemado(a)	44. scottatura	44. Queimado	44. Yakedo	44. pow

English	French	German	Spanish	Italian	Portuguese	Japanese	Thai
45. bus/terminal	45. Bus / terminal	45. Bus / Busbahnhof	45. autobús/terminal	45. autobus/terminale	45. Terminal de autocarros	45. Basu ta-aminaru	45. rot pra jum tahng
46. camp ground	46. Camping	46. Campingplatz	46. terreno del campamento	46. campeggio	46. Parque de campismo	46. Kyampu chi	46. kai tee pak
47. camera store	47. Magasin d'appareils photo	47. Fotohandlung	47. tienda de cámaras fotográficas	47. negozio di macchina fotografica	47. Loja de máquinas fotográficas	47. Kamera ya	47. rahn glorng tai roop
48. can opener	48. Ouvre-boîte	48. Dosenöffner	48. abridor de latas	48. apriscatole	48. Abre-latas	48. Kan kiri	48. tee pert graporng
49. candle	49. Bougie	49. Kerze	49. vela	49. candela	49. Vela	49. Ro-osoku	49. tee-an
50. currency exchange	50. Échange de devises	50. Wechselstube	50. cambio de moneda	50. cambio	50. Câmbio de moeda estrangeira	50. Ryo-o ga-e	50. lak ngerm
51. cheque	51. Chèque	51. Scheck	51. cheque	51. assegno bancario	51. Cheque	51. Kogitte	51. (ngern) check
52. cheese	52. Fromage	52. Käse	52. queso	52. formaggio	52. Queijo	52. Chi-izu	52. ner-y kaang
53. chicken	53. Poulet	53. Huhn	53. pollo	53. pollo	53. Frango	53. Chikin	53. gy
54. close	54. Près	54. schließen	54. cerca	54. vicino	54. Perto	54. Shimelu	54. pit
55. cold	55. Froid	55. kalt	55. frío	55. freddo	55. Frio	55. Samui	55. yen, noou
56. condoms	56. Préservatifs	56. Kondom.	56. condones	56. preservativi	56. Preservativos	56. Kondomu	56. toong yahng
57. dentist	57. Dentiste	57. Zahnarzt	57. dentista	57. dentista	57. Dentista	57. Haisha	57. mor fun
58. diabetic	58. Diabétique	58. Diabetiker	58. diabético(a)	58. diabetico	58. Diabético	58. To-onyo-byo-o	58. rok bow wahn
59. diarrhea	59. Diarrhée	59. Durchfall	59. diarrea	59. diarrea	59. Diarreia	59. Geli	59. torng roo-ang
60. dirty	60. Sale	60. schmutzig	60. sucio(a)	60. sporco	60. Sujo	60. Kitana-i	60. sok gaprok
61. doctor	61. Médecin	61. Arzt	61. doctor(a)	61. dottore	61. Médico	61. O-isha	61. mor, paat
62. egg	62. Oeuf	62. Ei	62. huevo	62. uovo	62. Ovo	62. Tamago	62. ky
63. embassy	63. Ambassade	63. Botschaft	63. embajada	63. ambasciata	63. Embaixada	63. Taishikan	63. tahn toot
64. envelope	64. Enveloppe	64. Briefumschlag	64. sobre	64. busta	64. Envelope	64. Fuuto-o	64. sorng, sorngjotmai
65. expensive	65. Cher	65. teuer	65. caro(a)	65. costoso	65. Dispendioso	65. Takai	65. paang
66. fan	66. Ventilateur	66. Ventilator	66. ventilador/aficionado	66. ventilatore	66. Ventoinha	66. Sensu	66. putlom
67. fast/slow	67. Rapide / lent	67. schnell / langsam	67. rápido(a)/lento(a)	67. veloce/lento	67. Rápido/lento	67. Hayaku/Yukkuri	67. rew / chah
68. ferry	68. Bac	68. Fähre	68. transbordador	68. traghetto	68. Ferry	68. Ferii	68. reu-a kahmfahk
69. fever	69. Fièvre	69. Fieber	69. fiebre	69. febbre	69. Febre	69. Netsu	69. ky
70. film	70. Film	70. Film	70. película	70. film	70. Rolo fotográfico	70. Fuirumu	70. film tai roop
71. fish	71. Poisson	71. Fisch	71. pescado	71. pesce	71. Peixe	71. Sakana	71. plah
72. flat tire	72. Crevaison	72. Plattfuß	72. rueda pinchada	72. pneumatico piatto	72. Pneu furado	72. Panku shimashita	72. yahng baah
73. fried	73. Frit	73. gebraten	73. frito(a)	73. fritto	73. Frito	73. Agemono	73. tort
74. fruit	74. Fruit	74. Obst	74. fruta	74. frutta	74. Fruta	74. Kudamono	74. pon-lamy
75. gasoline (petrol)	75. Essence	75. Benzin	75. gasolina	75. benzina (petrolio)	75. Gasolina	75. Gasolin	75. num mun ben sin
76. gift	76. Cadeau	76. Geschenk	76. regalo	76. regalo	76. Presente	76. Okurimono	76. korng kwun
77. grocery store	77. Épicier	77. Lebensmittelges-chäft	77. tienda de alimentos	77. negozio di generi alimentari	77. Mercearia	77. Su-upa-a	77. rahn kai korng
78. ham	78. Jambon	78. gekochter Schinken	78. jamón	78. prosciutto	78. Fiambre	78. Hamu	78. moo rom kwun
79. headache	79. Mal de tête	79. Kopfschmerzen	79. dolor de cabeza	79. mal di testa	79. Dor de cabeça	79. Zutsu-u	79. poo-at hoo-a
80. hotel	80. Hôtel	80. Hotel	80. hotel	80. albergo	80. Hotel	80. Hoteru	80. rong raam
81. hospital	81. Hôpital	81. Krankenhaus	81. hospital	81. ospedale	81. Hospital	81. Byo-o-in	81. rong pa yah bahn

English	French	German	Spanish	Italian	Portuguese	Japanese	Thai
82. hot	82. Chaud	82. heiß	82. caliente	82. caldo	82. Quente	82. Atsui	82. rorn
83. ice	83. Glace	83. Eis	83. hielo	83. ghiaccio	83. Gelo	83. Ko-o-ri	83. num kaang
84. ice cream	84. Glace	84. Eis	84. helado	84. gelato	84. Gelado	84. Aisukuri-i-mu	84. ice keam
85. information	85. Information	85. Auskunft	85. información	85. informazioni	85. Informação	85. Inho-me-e-shion	85. kaou
86. infection	86. Infection	86. Entzündung	86. infección	86. infezione	86. Infecção	86. Kan-sen	86. rok dtid ator
87. key	87. Clé	87. Schlüssel	87. llave	87. chiave	87. Chave	87. Kagi	87. look goonjaa
88. lamb	88. Agneau	88. Lamm	88. cordero	88. agnello	88. Borrego	88. Lamu	88. look gaa
89. lamp	89. Lampe	89. Lampe	89. lámpara	89. lampada	89. Candeiro	89. Lamu	89. dta gee-ang
90. laundry	90. Lessive	90. Wäsche	90. ropa para lavar	90. lavanderia	90. Lavandaria	90. Sentaku	90. suk reed
91. laxative	91. Laxatif	91. Abführmittel	91. laxante	91. lassativo	91. Laxativo	91. Gezai	91. ya ra bai
92. letter/stamp	92. Lettre / timbre	92. Brief / Briefmarke	92. carta/sello postal	92. lettera/francobollo	92. Carta/selo	92. Tegami/Kitte	92. jotmai / sadtaamp
93. locker	93. Casier	93. Schließfach	93. armario	93. armadietto	93. Cacifo	93. Lokka-a	93. dtoo
94. mail	94. Courrier	94. Post	94. correo	94. posta	94. Correio	94. Yu-ubin butsu	94. pry sa nee
95. map	95. Carte	95. Landkarte	95. mapa	95. mappa	95. Mapa	95. Chizu	95. paan tee
96. market	96. Marché	96. Markt	96. mercado	96. mercato	96. Mercado	96. Ma-a-ketto	96. dtalaht
97. medicine	97. Médecine	97. Medizin	97. medicina	97. medicina	97. Medicamento	97. Kusuri	97. yah
98. milk	98. Lait	98. Milch	98. leche	98. latte	98. Leite	98. Miluku	98. num nom
99. money	99. Argent	99. Geld	99. dinero	99. denaro	99. Dinheiro	99. Okane	99. ngern
100. museum	100. Musée	100. Museum	100. museo	100. museo	100. Museu	100. Bijutsukan	100. pipi-tapunsatahn
101. nausea	101. Nausée	101. Übelkeit	101. náusea	101. nausea	101. Náusea	101. Hakke	101. kleun ngee-an
102. net (bed)	102. Hamac	102. Netz	102. mosquitero (cama)	102. letto	102. Cama de rede	102. Netto (beddo)	102. rahng haa
103. newspaper	103. Journal	103. Zeitung	103. diario	103. giornale	103. Jornal	103. Shimbun	103. nungseupim
104. oil (automobile)	104. Huile	104. Öl	104. aceite (automóvil)	104. olio (automobile)	104. Óleo (automóvel)	104. O-i-lu	104. num mun rot
105. open	105. Ouvert	105. geöffnet	105. abrir	105. aperto	105. Aberto	105. Akeru	105. pert
106. pharmacy	106. Pharmacie	106. Apotheke	106. farmacia	106. farmacia	106. Farmácia	106. Yakkyoku	106. rahn kai ya
107. pen	107. Plume	107. Stift	107. bolígrafo	107. penna	107. Caneta	107. Pen	107. pahk gah
108. pepper	108. Poivre	108. Pfeffer	108. pimienta	108. pepe	108. Pimenta	108. Pepaa	108. prik ty
109. police	109. Police	109. Polizei	109. policía	109. polizia	109. Policia	109. Keisatsu	109. dtumroo-at
110. pork	110. Porc	110. Schweinefleisch	110. cerdo	110. carne di maiale	110. Carne de porco	110. Po-oku	110. neu-a moo
111. post-card	111. carte postale	111. Postkarte	111. tarjeta postal	111. cartolina	111. Postal ilustrado	111. Ehagaki	111. pry sa nee ya bat
112. post office	112. Bureau de poste	112. Postamt	112. oficina de correos	112. ufficio postale	112. Estação de correios	112. Yu-ubinkyoku	112. tee tum kahn pry sa nee
113. press (iron)	113. Repassage	113. bügeln	113. planchar (plancha)	113. stirare (ferro da stiro)	113. Vincar (com o ferro)	113. Airon kakeru	113. reet pah
114. rare (meat)	114. Saignant	114. nicht durchgebraten	114. cruda (carne)	114. al sangue/poco cotto	114. Carne mal passada	114. Sukoshi yaita niku	114. my sook mahk
115. rice	115. Beau	115. nett	115. bonito(a)	115. gentile	115. Bonito	115. Gohan	115. dee, soo-ay
116. reservation	116. Réservation	116. Reservierung	116. reservación	116. prenotazione	116. Reserva	116. Yoyaku	116. putdtahkahn
117. room	117. Pièce	117. Zimmer	117. habitación	117. camera	117. Quarto	117. Heya	117. horng
118. salt	118. Sel	118. Salz	118. sal	118. sale	118. Sal	118. Shio	118. gleu-a
119. sandwich	119. Sandwich	119. Butterbrot	119. sandwich	119. panino	119. Sanduiche	119. Sando icchi	119. kanom pung sandwich

English	French	German	Spanish	Italian	Portuguese	Japanese	Thai
120. shower	120. Douche	120. Dusche	120. ducha	120. doccia	120. Banho de chuveiro	120. Shawaa	120. aahm num
121. sick	121. Malade	121. krank	121. enfermo(a)	121. malato	121. Doente	121. Byo-o-ki	121. poo-ay, mysa bai
122. smoking	122. Fumeur	122. rauchen	122. fumar	122. fumare	122. Fumar	122. Kitsu-en	122. soop boo ree
123. soap	123. Savon	123. Seife	123. jabón	123. sapone	123. Sabonete	123. Sekken	123. sa boo]
124. sore	124. Douloureux	124. tut weh	124. dolore	124. dolente	124. Ferida	124. Kizu	124. jeb
125. stop	125. Arrêt	125. halt, stopp	125. pare	125. fermare	125. Pare	125. Tomaru/Tomeru	125. yoot
126. student discount	126. Tarif étudiant	126. Studentenrabatt	126. descuento para estudiantes	126. sconto per studente	126. Desconto para estudantes	126. Gakuse-e waribiki	126. raka nuk ree-an
127. subway (metro)	127. Métro	127. U-Bahn	127. metro	127. metropolitana	127. Metropolitano	127. Chikatetsu	127. rot fy dty din (ny krung)
128. sugar	128. Sucre	128. Zucker	128. azúcar	128. zucchero	128. Açúcar	128. Satoo	128. num dtahn
129. tampons	129. Tampon	129. Tampons	129. tampones	129. tamponi	129. Tampão	129. Tampon	129. pah anamai lohd
130. taxi	130. Taxi	130. Taxi	130. taxi	130. tassi	130. Táxi	130. Takushi-i	130. (rot) taaksee
131. tea	131. Thé	131. Tee	131. té	131. tè	131. Chá	131. Ko-ocha	131. num chah
132. telephone	132. Téléphone	132. Telefon	132. teléfono	132. telefono	132. Telefone	132. Denwa	132. torasup
133. ticket (travel)	133. Billet	133. Fahrkarte, Flugkarte	133. billete (viaje)	133. biglietto (viaggiare)	133. Bilhete de viagem	133. Kippu	133. atoo-a (dern tahng)
134. ticket office	134. Centre des billets	134. Kartenverkauf	134. taquilla	134. biglietteria	134. Escritório de venda de bilhetes	134. Kippu uriba	134. atoo-a sumnuk ngahn
135. tissues	135. Tissu	135. Papierta-schentüch-er	135. pañuelos de papel	135. tessuto	135. Lenços de papel	135. Chishu-u	135. gradaht chet meu
136. toilet	136. Toilette	136. Toilette	136. los servicios	136. toletta	136. Casa de banho	136. Ote arai	136. horn num
137. toilet paper	137. Papier hygiénique	137. Toilettenpapier	137. papel higiénico	137. carta igienica	137. Papel higiénico	137. Toiretto pe-epaa	137. gradaht horng num
138. tooth ache	138. Mal de dent	138. Zähnschmerzen	138. dolor de muelas	138. mal di denti	138. Dor de dentes	138. Haga i-tai	138. poo-at fun
139. today	139. Aujourd'hui	139. heute	139. hoy	139. oggi	139. Hoje	139. Kyo-o	139. wun nee
140. tomorrow	140. Demain	140. morgen	140. mañana	140. domani	140. Amanhã	140. Ashita	140. proong nee
141. towel	141. Serviette	141. Handtuch	141. toalla	141. asciugamano	141. Toalha	141. Taoru	141. par chet too-a
142. train station	142. Gare	142. Bahnhof	142. estación de ferro-carril	142. stazione di treni	142. Estação de com-boios	142. Eki	142. satahnee rotfy
143. up/down	143. En haut / en bas	143. hoch / runter	143. arriba/abajo	143. sopra/sotto	143. Para cima/para baixo	143. Ue/Shita	143. keun / long
144. vegetables	144. Légumes	144. Gemüse	144. verduras	144. verdura	144. Vegetais	144. Yasai	144. puk
145. vegetarian	145. Végétarien	145. Vegetarier	145. vegetariano(a)	145. vegetariano	145. Vegetariano	145. Saishoku shugi-sha	145. gin jay
146. visa	146. Visa	146. Visum	146. visa	146. visto	146. Visto	146. Biza	146. nungseu dern tahng
147. waiting room	147. Salle d'attente	147. Wartezimmer	147. sala de atesa	147. sala d'attesa	147. Sala de espera	147. Machiai shitsu	147. horng puk
148. water (bottled)	148. Eau de source	148. Mineralwasser	148. agua (embotellada)	148. acqua pottabile	148. Água engarrafada	148. Bin iri no mizu	148. num
149. wine	149. Vin	149. Wein	149. vino	149. vino	149. Vinho	149. wain	149. num wine
150. youth hostel	150. Auberge de jeunesse	150. Jugendherberge	150. albergue juvenil	150. ostello della gioven-tù	150. Albergue para jovens	150. Yuusu hosuteru	150. horpuk sumrup dek

METRIC CONVERSIONS

centimeters	cm/inches	inches
2.54	1	0.39
5.08	2	0.79
7.62	3	1.18
10.16	4	1.58
12.70	5	1.97
15.24	6	2.36
17.78	7	2.76
20.32	8	3.15
22.86	9	3.54
25.40	10	3.94
63.50	25	9.84

kilograms	kg/pounds	pounds
0.45	1	2.20
0.91	2	4.41
1.36	3	6.61
1.81	4	8.82
2.27	5	11.02
2.72	6	13.23
3.18	7	15.43
3.63	8	17.64
4.08	9	19.84
4.54	10	22.05
9.07	20	44.09
13.61	30	66.14
18.14	40	88.19
22.68	50	110.20

metres	metres/feet	feet/inches
.30	1	3'3"
60	2	6'7"
0.91	3	9'9"
1.22	4	13'2"
1.53	5	16'3"
3.04	10	32'6"
7.62	25	82'
15.24	50	164'
30.48	100	328'

CEL.	TO	FAH.
-05	—	23
-04	—	24
-03	—	26
-02	—	28
-01	—	30
0	—	32.0
01	—	33.8
02	—	35.6
03	—	37.4
04	—	39.2
05	—	41.0
06	—	42.8
07	—	44.6
08	—	46.4
09	—	48.2
10	—	50.0
11	—	51.8
12	—	53.6
13	—	55.4
14	—	57.2
15	—	59.0
16	—	60.8
17	—	62.6
18	—	64.4
19	—	66.2
20	—	68.0
21	—	69.8
22	—	71.6
23	—	73.4
24	—	75.2
25	—	77.0
26	—	78.8
27	—	80.6
28	—	82.4
29	—	84.2
30	—	86.8

litres	litres/US gal	US gal
3.79	1	0.26
7.57	2	0.53
11.36	3	0.79
15.14	4	1.06
18.93	5	1.32
22.71	6	1.59
26.50	7	1.85
30.28	8	2.11
34.07	9	2.38
37.85	10	2.64
75.70	20	5.28
113.60	30	7.93
151.40	40	10.57
189.30	50	13.21
378.54	100	26.41

kilometres	km/miles	miles
1.61	1	0.62
3.22	2	1.24
4.83	3	1.86
6.44	4	2.49
8.05	5	3.11
9.66	6	3.73
11.27	7	4.35
12.88	8	4.97
14.48	9	5.59
16.09	10	6.21
32.19	20	12.43
48.28	30	18.64
64.37	40	24.86
80.47	50	31.07
160.93	100	62.13

litres	litres/Imp.gal	gal
4.54	1	0.22
9.09	2	0.44
13.63	3	0.66
18.18	4	1.10
22.73	5	1.09
27.27	6	1.31
31.82	7	1.53
36.36	8	1.75
40.91	9	1.97
45.46	10	2.20
90.92	20	4.39
136.38	30	6.59
181.84	40	8.79
227.30	50	10.99
454.60	100	21.99

grams	g/oz	ounces
28	1	.03
57	2	.07
85	3	.10
113	4	.14
142	5	.17
283	10	0.35
567	20	0.70
850	30	1.05
1,417	50	1.75
2,835	100	3.50
14,175	500	17.63

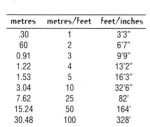

Name   Telephone/E-Mail

Address

Name   Telephone/E-Mail

Address

Name   Telephone/E-Mail

Address

Name   Telephone/E-Mail

Address

Name   Telephone/E-Mail

Address

Name   Telephone/E-Mail

Address

Name   Telephone/E-Mail

Address

Name   Telephone/E-Mail

Address

Name   Telephone/E-Mail

Address

Name   Telephone/E-Mail

Address

Name   Telephone/E-Mail

Address

Name   Telephone/E-Mail

Address

Name   Telephone/E-Mail

Address

Name   Telephone/E-Mail

Address

Name   Telephone/E-Mail

Address

Name   Telephone/E-Mail

Address

Name   Telephone/E-Mail

Address

Name   Telephone/E-Mail

Address

Name   Telephone/E-Mail

Address

Name   Telephone/E-Mail

Address

Name   Telephone/E-Mail

Address

Name   Telephone/E-Mail

Address

Name   Telephone/E-Mail

Address

Name   Telephone/E-Mail

Address

Name   Telephone/E-Mail

Address

Name   Telephone/E-Mail

Address

Name   Telephone/E-Mail

Address

Name   Telephone/E-Mail

Address

Name   Telephone/E-Mail

Address

Name   Telephone/E-Mail

Address

Your gateway to Backpacker Information on the Internet
Izon's Backpacker Journal
www.izon.com

If you have a tip or tale you'd like to contribute to Izon's
Backpacker Journal, write to P.O. Box 1043, Station Q, Toronto,
Canada M4V 1J7 or e-mail izon@compuserve.com. Postcards with helpful
tips will be displayed on www.izon.com.
Watch for the latest news on backpacking around the world on the
Backpacker News Wire at www.izon.com.

Izon's Backpacker Journal makes a great gift. Order a copy for a friend.
Call Ten Speed Press toll-free (800) 841-2665.

The information presented is not intended to be a
substitute for professional medical treatment. I
encourage you to seek medical advice before you
travel and, if necessary, during your journey;
also invest in a detailed guidebook (it will be
well worth the weight). I highly recommend the
authors whose quotes have been included.

With thanks to:

Dr. Philip Scappatura, M.D. CCFP,
Travel Inoculation Clinic,
Toronto General Hospital.

Dr. Authur Dunec, D.D.S.